CAER

D1374471

Slideshow

Slideshow

Slideshow

Memories of a Wartime Childhood

Marjorie Ann Watts

QUARTET

First published in 2014 by Quartet Books Limited
A member of the Namara Group
27 Goodge Street, London W1T 2LD
Copyright © Marjorie Ann Watts 2014
The right of Marjorie Ann Watts to be identified
as the author of this work has been asserted
by her in accordance with the
Copyright, Designs and Patents Act, 1988
All rights reserved.
No part of this book may be reproduced in
any form or by any means without prior
written permission from the publisher
A catalogue record for this book
is available from the British Library
ISBN 978 0 7043 7359 4
Typeset by Josh Bryson
Printed and bound in Great Britain by
T J International Ltd, Padstow, Cornwall

For my mother

Preface

The needs of Empire and two world wars only twenty years apart, vagaries of temperament, accidental death, whatever the reason – in our English twentieth-century childhood, fathers and grandfathers, uncles, even male cousins, were thin on the ground.

There were glimpses of my father – before he disappeared when I was eight – but for me he was a remote and forbidding figure, and we didn't know him in the sense that a majority of modern British children know their 'Dad' nowadays. At the time and in my parent's milieu, this was common; which is frustrating, as by all accounts he was a charmer. Talented, cultivated, good-looking, adored by wife and intimates alike, at social events or amongst friends he was an attractive and amusing man. But like many people who have to be funny professionally – he was a black and white cartoonist for *Punch* and other magazines – at home he could be moody and depressive. (Always afraid his cartoons would suddenly become 'unfunny', and work would dry up.) Also he did not much like children. My mother maintained that war had changed him: in World War One, after astonishing bravery as a commander in the Royal Naval Reserve, he was discharged decorated, but badly shell-shocked. They had ten years of happy marriage, then having escaped death in war, he was killed at only fifty-two in a civil air disaster in 1935. Four years later, Hitler's panzers roared into Poland, and my mother was left facing World War Two, with debts and three young children.

My paternal grandfather, an army officer in India during the heyday of the Raj, succumbed to yellow fever a few months before my father was born. And my other grandfather, my mother's father – a general practitioner descended from a long line of Indian army doctors and surgeon-generals – joined up as an army doctor at the beginning of the First World War, but after it had ended became depressed and committed suicide. All in all, a couple of uncles (my mother's brothers), not much of a father, and no grandfathers: a dearth of adult males. Great aunts and grandmothers were more in evidence.

Hampstead, where we lived until the outbreak of World War Two, was completely unfashionable at that time, an area which – when seen from wealthy and well-born Belgravia, or cheaper Bloomsbury – was 'too far out' and therefore undesirable.

'Your little bohemian cul-de-sac on the edge of primeval forest' is how my father's friend E.M. Delafield described Holly Place on a postcard in 1926.

She was joking, of course, but Hampstead then was more like a village or miniature country town than the wealthy tourist hot spot it has become today. Well-proportioned detached houses set back from the road – in gardens backing on to tenement buildings, the Victorian hospital, old poor house; winding narrow streets of small terraced cottages, two-up-two-down, no bathroom, a galvanised bath hanging on the back of a shed door, a privy in the tiny yard, and a rent of a few shillings a month – all eagerly gentrified today. Or, perhaps on the edge of the Heath, glimpsed through a half-open gate – a few grander establishments screened by trees and shrubs or ancient walls, coach houses now transformed into garages or artisan premises. And working stables! In the Hampstead of my early childhood, a variety of horses could be seen every day, pulling brewery drays, costermongers' rattling little carts, milk floats up and down the steep hills. Instead of the traffic noise and screech of police and ambulance sirens of today, the air was full of the sing-song chatter of children. Either from various schools and orphanages – children of recently dead soldiers from World War One dotted about – or the streets and pavements where children of all ages skipped and chatted, played tag and hopscotch, the complicated counting games that the majority of ordinary children of the period knew: side roads and back streets were relatively safe to play in then, as few people had cars. Perhaps one of the biggest changes to the Hampstead of the present time, though, is that, in those days, the butcher, the baker, the chemist, florist, haberdasher, painter and decorator – even the errand boy – all lived just around the corner probably in one of the now gentrified two-up-two-downs, and walked to work nearby.

However, economic circumstances for many at the time were dire. Unemployment, poverty, wretched housing and lack of health care, not to mention the rigid class distinctions, made life cruelly harsh and unpredictable for large numbers of people. And soon after I was born, ominous storm clouds were already gathering on a not-so-distant horizon.

Although cocooned in a kind of security, as a small child I seem to have been aware of a certain 'thin ice' quality inherent in being alive and, Eeyore-like, was known for expecting the worst. Ironically, when it happened and disaster actually struck, life seemed to improve – for me anyway.

Things might not have turned out so well, however, if we had not had the mother we did. Quite a lot of our childhood was during wartime, but she seldom admitted to fear, and we took our cue from her. Life was exciting, full of interest and possibilities. We were never bored, never felt the lack of money (which undoubtedly existed), or that we were circumscribed, not good or brave enough,

3

could not confront and surmount obstacles – catastrophe even. And when I observe the constrained life of many children in Britain today – often overweight, bored, dazzled by celebrity and advertising, addicted to drugs or computer gaming and dependent on someone to drive them somewhere, anywhere but where they are – I think back to the freedom and excitement, the challenging kaleidoscopic landscape of my childhood, and am grateful. We were very lucky, of course. While millions suffered and died, England was not invaded or occupied.

Born at the turn of the century, my mother claimed that she had been held up to the window by her mother to see the funeral cortège of Queen Victoria pass by. And that may have been true as, at the time, her father was a junior doctor in the practice, which looked after the children and servants at Buckingham Palace, and the family lived a few minutes' walk from the Mall.

Initially, her childhood was conventional enough: two brothers, her mother, and a father now with a busy doctor's practice of his own; an ordinary middle-class scenario. But all that changed when her mother – Amy Dawson-Scott, a freethinker and feminist and by then an established writer – had one of her bright 'ideas', and founded International PEN.*

---

* International PEN is a non-governmental organisation founded in 1921 by Amy Dawson-Scott. Its aims were:

1. To promote intellectual co-operation and understanding among writers.
2. To create an international community of writers that would emphasise the central role of literature in the development of world culture.
3. To defend literature against the many threats to its survival that the modern world poses.

The first president was John Galsworthy. Joseph Conrad, Elizabeth Craig, George Bernard Shaw, and H.G. Wells were among its first members.

'Your father married me because I am an optimist!' my mother would sometimes say to me. 'I inherited it from Grandma.'

I am sure that this was so, although optimist as Grandma clearly was, at close quarters she was definitely not the easiest of people.

My father is reported as saying that when his mother-in-law was in the house, he felt as if he was in a railway station where, somehow, he was always on the wrong platform. In fact she was not in the house very often, as they did not get on and anyway she was far too busy to spend much time with any of her immediate family. Her energy was prodigious. She wrote twenty novels and a fair amount of poetry, all published, as well as coping with the multifarious organisational activities and committee work necessary to initiate and then keep PEN up and running. Eccentric and somewhat quick tempered, she was an Edwardian when it came to etiquette and manners. Children, and also daughter's husbands, would have been expected to tread softly and do as she told them. (Unlikely, in the case of my father.)

My mother was in at the start of the 'PEN Club' as it was known in the beginning, as its secretary. She soon showed that she, too, was an accomplished organiser, and helped with the minutiae and planning involved in PEN's social events, mostly dinners; who was to be invited, who would sit next to whom, who should be encouraged and cosseted, or not. And like her mother she could be forceful.

'It's so inconvenient…why are you always so late?' she is reputed to have asked Beatrice Webb, famous for bad timekeeping, guest of honour on this occasion but so late that she arrived with the soup.

5

'Well, I-I have to er…I have to wash Sydney's socks!' Mrs Webb is said to have replied.

That must have been when my mother was a girl in her early twenties. Fifteen or so years later, widowed and without qualifications apart from a secretarial course at eighteen, she earned her living at a variety of jobs, endured six years of war, brought up three children, and then at fifty went back to college and took a social science degree before training as a children's probation officer. It was a job she loved and was so good at that she was asked to continue after official retirement – which she did until she was seventy-five. She remained passionately committed to PEN, however, and later on when things started up again after the war, took an intense and practical interest in a now worldwide organisation, sitting on the executive committee of English PEN until she was well into her nineties.

Amusing stories and gossip about this or that distinguished but difficult novelist or poet, about publishers, translators, editors, scandals, the malfunctioning or achievements of this or that PEN centre, therefore circulated freely in my home – especially after my father had died. Taking it all completely for granted, of course, we were mildly entertained, sometimes even interested. For instance, aged about eleven I can clearly remember sitting between Henry Williamson of *Tarka the Otter* fame, and J.B. Priestly, discussing whether limpets were edible, how to determine whether mussels were poisonous and the best places to find and cook them. (On the beach in Cornwall in the winter, according to Henry Williamson, having been hacked from the surrounding rocks.)

The capacity to remember events, faces, names, places, conversations, varies from person to person, of course, and there are many different kinds of memory. Visual memory and perhaps the absence of memory for anything to do with number or arithmetic are the ones I know most about.

As a book illustrator, I have drawn objects and people, animals, landscapes and scenes of various kinds since I could hold a pencil and at one time could probably have produced all these things to order – from observation. But also, for a very long time I have had a store of 'slides' or pictures of past events and people in my mind which are bright and clear, and unchanging. Perhaps everyone does? All I have to do is pull out a 'slide' from the accumulated silt of memory laid down through the years, and concentrate – 'really look', as my father advised. And there it is: a varnish-clear image as vivid as the day it was first recorded, however long ago. And for me, once the visual scene has been presented to the inner eye, the words associated with it come tripping back as if triggered by the image. If I can see the face, the hat, the street, the scene of perhaps forty or fifty, even eighty years ago, usually I can hear the conversation attached. The fragments presented here, therefore, are taken from this store of bright intense images amassed over a long life, and the events they conjure up. Initially brief and relatively uncomplicated, later a combination of recollections and snapshot images, which become more sophisticated and dense as time passes, but no less vivid; a sort of slideshow recalling a vanished world and some of the people in it.

On the whole, children are accustomed to the mother they have, and like other children we were used to ours. Since retrieving my 'slides', however, and thinking about her life and the predicament she found herself in, I find myself marvelling at what a truly remarkable woman she was. Left on her own with three young children at the beginning of an all-encompassing war – short of money and alone – she not only survived magnificently but saw to it somehow that her children did, too.

Gentler than her own mother, more subtle in her understanding and appreciation of people, especially children, her fortitude, qualities of courage and ingenuity, determination, and sheer stamina amazed everyone who knew her. To this day, how she coped with whatever was thrown at her continues to astonish me. For her children, the early violent death of a father, the Blitz, the blackout, sirens wailing, doodlebugs, food rationing and shortages of just about everything, the shadow of fear and death – not to mention no television or computer games, indeed no mobile phones or cyber space or convenient car trips – were the background to our growing-up years. And it sometimes surprises me that we were as happy and resilient as we were. Yet children usually accept what is. We were lucky in our gallant, strong-willed, optimistic mother, and skated along somehow avoiding disaster.

Sitting in my study looking out over the leafy graveyard where my parents are buried, and only a few hundred yards from where I was born, on the whole I still think of it as an exciting, rewarding and often happy time – fragments of which I hope I have captured in what follows.

Hampstead, London, May 2014

I
1927–1939
Holly Place, Hampstead

Green lawns spreading towards dark trees striping the grass. The garden of Great Aunt Maud at Fleet.

Rose petals fall without a sound, dropping on top of me. People are talking but I can't see them, only bunches of roses hanging pink and white against a blue sky. Great Aunt Maude smells like old dried-out paper.

Mackintosh and rain, black umbrellas, rain drops. I am looking down Holly Hill, out past grey nanny Kathleen's face (grey hat, grey hair, grey uniform), the crinkled edges of the pram hood.

'Such a big heavy girl…I can't get you to the top of the hill,' she says, laughing as she pushes me up the steep slope.

1930

Blue curling dragons, their fierce angry faces and tails ending in sprays of flowers, patterning the nursery sofa. They are growling at me, so I growl back. Behind the sofa and the curtain is the bed where I sleep. Kathleen sleeps there too in another bed. She holds the baby out for me to see; Simon, a poor limp little thing in a long dress and knitted clothes too big for him. No hair. She shows me the soft place in his head where you can see his heart beating, and I am sorry for him because he is so small and ugly. Mumma comes in with an apron on, and there is a lot

9

of fuss and noise while he is undressed and washed in a special bath on two chairs. He turns a horrid red colour and screams and screams, but I don't take any notice. Why do they like him so much?

The grocer's shop is like a palace. The floor is black and white stone diamonds and our footsteps echo as we walk. Reflections follow us along the walls. Mumma is wearing her blue frock and hat with the flowers and is holding my hand. If I stand on my toes, I can see the gold and pink weighing machines, shiny gold weights, baskets of eggs, and, along the cold top of the marble counter, creamy yellow blocks of butter like tall buildings. Above our heads, hams and pieces of bacon hang from a rail up near the ceiling. A tall thin man in a black overall with white crinkled cuffs, stiff white collar and a long starched apron is waiting: Mr Smeeton, the manager. He takes a pencil from behind his ear, and says, 'The order'm…certainly'm. Yes'm, this afternoon'm,' then he speaks very quickly and crossly to one of the little boys making butter pats with a grooved wooden paddle thing. His hands are red, raw, too big for his arms somehow, and he bumps and scrapes his boots on the diamond floor as if they are too heavy. Later he will ride up the hill on a bicycle with two dozen eggs, bacon and some butter all packed into a basket in the front. I ask if he can come and play when he brings it. Nobody answers. I wish I had a bicycle.

Sometimes we go to Ankerman's, the butcher. The strings of sausages hanging up are all right, but he has calves' heads and their tongues on dishes, and red shiny liver – what is liver? Worst of all are the poor rabbits, their soft fur dribbled with blood, eyes staring out sideways at you. They have bloody slits in their stomachs and are tied

10

together in pairs. I feel so sorry for them, but Mumma says don't be silly, they are dead. Then there is the fishmonger, Mr Knockles. He wears a striped apron too, and a straw boater. One of his arms ends in a hook, and all his fish look at you with their fishy dead eyes as if they want to say something.

There is a different nanny now, Fat Nanny. I love her very much. She wears a rustling pale blue uniform with a stiff white belt and sometimes a floaty white veil thing. She never gets cross. Today I pinched her and said she was a fat pig, and she just smiled and picked me up and put me on her lap. She has a nice soft cushiony place on her front called a bosom. We go out on the Heath with the other nannies in their different coloured uniforms: pale blue, dark blue, mauve, white, like butterflies. My nanny is the best of all.

Upstairs in our house, cook is shouting in the kitchen.

'Cook is as cross as two sticks today,' Nanny says, putting the tray with our steaming dinner on it down on the nursery table with a bang. What does she mean, two cross sticks?

'It means somebody who got out of bed the wrong side,' Nanny says. 'Sit up straight dear.'

One of the nursery doors leads out into a big yard where the dustbins are, and the back of the Catholic church. The other opens on to stairs that go from the nursery at the bottom, past the hall and the front door, up through the house to the drawing room, and then the bedrooms. Up more narrow creaking stairs, and into the studio – a big high room that belongs to Father. He is very, very tall – that is why the studio is so high. I have to be quiet and behave properly when I am there because he is 'working'. He is an artist and draws all day. (Working means earning money, Nanny says.) Sometimes Mumma takes me up to the studio and reads a story while he draws me. I have to stand still and not wriggle, but usually he says, 'That child is like a jack-in-a-box!' – although I am trying my best. Sometimes after tea, I have to go up with Nanny to say goodnight to him. I can't see his face, he is so tall, but he has shiny brown polished shoes where I can see my reflection, so I look at those instead. Simon is too little to come upstairs yet.

'I don't want to say goodnight,' I tell Nanny while she brushes my hair. But all she says is:

'Look at those fingernails…are we in mourning for the cat? Keep still dear.'

Coke and coal are kept outside the nursery: you can smell it in the cellars on either side of the stairs there. I can open the little triangle which is a door and get in, but it is black. I did this once, but I got coal on my dress and everyone was cross. I was smacked and put in the bath with very hot water. The coalmen come with their bags of coal, and pour it through a hole in the pavement outside, then Rose can do the fires. Rose sleeps somewhere near the front door, I am not sure where. When I am ill, she makes a fire in a room upstairs next to Mumma's room, and I lie in bed and the doctor comes.

Mumma is sad today. Nanny says it is because Great Aunt Maude has passed away and is safe in the arms of Jesus – who *is* Jesus? At bedtime, I ask Mumma about Great Aunt Maude. She says she was Grandfather's older sister, and when he was a little boy sent back from India to grow up she looked after him, and he didn't see his mother again for

12

seventeen years. I start crying because I don't want to be sent away to live somewhere else for seventeen years. But Mumma laughs and says don't be a silly goose, I am not sending you anywhere.

The coalmen's horses are black like the coalmen, only their eyes are white. The brewery horses are brown, enormous, with long, light-coloured swishing tails and manes, feathery plumes round their hooves. I saw four of them today, pulling the beer dray right into the middle of the Whitestone Pond and drinking the water while the brewery man washed them and the cart. The milkman's horse stands outside our gate munching oats from the bag over his nose and rattling his harness, waiting to be given a sugar lump. Mumma tells me to hold my hand out flat so it will be easy for him to get it, but I don't like those big wet yellow teeth. She says he won't hurt me, but I don't believe her. With all those *teeth*?

Grandma is taking me and Mumma to a theatre to see a play, *Where the Rainbow Ends*. I have to wear my velvet dress and dancing shoes, and have my hair washed and a ribbon. Mumma says isn't it kind of her, it's a treat. Actually I would rather go swimming.

I am never going to go to another play as long as I live. (Nanny says I am a poor lamb and I don't have to.) The place where the rainbow ends is a horrible silvery green castle where two poor children have been taken by the Dragon King. He is a sort of greenish metal colour as well, and has wings and a long scaly tail. I am not sure what he is going to do to the children, but something bad, eat them probably. Anyway, I don't know what happens in the end, because when he says he is going to push them off the castle wall and dash their brains out, I get under my seat and shut my eyes. Mumma keeps saying 'it's all right, stop crying, everything is going to end happily', but I don't come out from under the seat. Grandma says I am such a baby, she is going to take Simon next time.

Today when we go for a walk, there is straw on the road. It is to make it quiet for an ill lady in our street. When she is dead, she is put in the graveyard under the ground with a stone on top of her. We walk past the graveyard almost every day. Simon is in his pram, so he is quite safe, but I think about all the dead people under their stones. What would happen if one of them pushed very hard and got out? Stretched their long thin arms through the railings? Nanny says that once you're in there, you never come out again because you're dead. I am not going to let that happen to me.

Sometimes Nanny laughs and calls me her Little Miss Scissors. She says I am so sharp I will cut myself one day. What does she mean?

1932

It is summer and we are in the dicky of the car going to Cornwall. It is a long way, days and days. On the way there, we have to stay the night in a feather bed. In Cornwall, the water outside the windows stretches away like a shining silver plate – to where the sea is, I think. Under the water, thick black mud sucks at your feet. We get black 'boots' and 'stockings' when we walk in it at low tide looking for cockles and little crabs no bigger than your fingernail. The boy at the mill found a huge long worm in the mud, and cut it in half. Then he cut the two halves in half, and those bits in half again, and they all wriggled about in the mud as if they were enjoying it.

When the tide is high, cold salty water from the sea comes swishing in over the top of the dam and fills up the mill pond so we can swim. We are not allowed in Father's boat.

In the morning, everybody except Father goes to pick blackberries in the quarry field. Then Mumma and my half-sister Margaret make jam. I am in the kitchen watching them, and two, then three, four, five black and yellow wasps drop into the huge steaming pan full of boiling jam. They squirm around for a bit, but they never get out. I don't feel sad for wasps.

We often go to the beach in Cornwall, and I run very fast across the sand into the sea and jump over the waves. I love it. I wish I could live in the sea always like a fish or a seal. When we come out of the water we usually have pieces of chocolate or a picnic. Father always says 'have a sand-sandwich, Marjorie' to my mother (that's her name), as a joke. Or, 'My God, this beach is big enough! Go and dig somewhere else, children.'

A family of old sisters, the Miss Marleys live up the lane at Melingey, seven of them – Miss Gertrude, Miss Kathleen, Miss Liza, Miss Jane and I can't remember the others. Miss Kathleen has a moustache and black hairs growing out of her chin. She does the cooking. Miss Gertrude is fat, with a loud voice and ho, ho, ho laugh. She looks after all the animals, chickens, ducks, peacocks, the geese and a small shaggy pony in the long field by the river. She waddles when she walks like one of her geese. Mrs Marley their mother is a hundred and stays in bed upstairs. Today, we are visiting them all for tea.

Melingey House is next door to a flour mill – where everything, windows, doors, the ground outside, even the miller himself standing on a little platform high up on the very tall building, is all covered with white flour dust. He is seeing to sacks full of flour being lowered down and then loaded on to a cart standing in the yard below him. That's all white too. At the back of the mill, water swirls along a leat, falls on to a huge creaking wheel, goes round a few times and then drops down and disappears under the house. Comes out again on the other side. When we visit, Miss Gertrude sometimes pulls up a thick heavy floor slate in the hall, and shows us the black water rushing past under the floor.

'That's where we put naughty children,' she says. I don't think she means it…does she?

The dining room table is covered by a maroon-coloured velvet cloth with bobbles round the edge, and a white lace cloth over that. Tea is spread out on it: chocolate cake, saffron bread, a lemon sponge, fish paste sandwiches, shortbread, splits and cream with strawberry jam. The teapot has a cosy made in the shape of an old-fashioned lady in a crinoline; and there are soft-boiled eggs with toast fingers, and homemade fizzy lemonade for the children. Miss Jane cuts off the top of her egg with a little silver chopper thing called John the Baptist, and Miss Katherine says to me, 'Kindly pass the Baptist, child.' After tea, we have to go upstairs to say good afternoon to old Mrs Marley. She is a little tiny person like a doll lying in the middle of a soft billowing white bed. The light coming into the room through the lace curtains is so dim and shadowy that all you can see properly are her eyes gleaming in her old face.

Miss Gertrude doesn't come in to tea; she has to see to her 'girls', she says. (She means the geese.) After tea, we go with her to see if the chickens have laid any eggs and the geese follow us about hissing and nipping at what they can get at, so I don't like them very much. Miss Gertrude laughs her ho, ho, ho laugh and says, 'Yes, pretty devilish aren't they, but they taste good.' Does she eat them then? And what about the pony? They can't eat *him*…can they?

While we are walking back to our house carrying a basket full of brown eggs and pieces of leftover Marley cake, Mumma tells us that Dr Marley, the Miss Marleys' father, was the great-great-great-grandson of a friend of her favourite writer, Charles Dickens. One day she will read his books to us. (My grandma is a writer too.) When we get home, Simon shows me some red velvet bobbles that he has pulled off the table cloth without anybody seeing.

Today Father is sailing his boat, *Summer Haze*, out to the sandbanks in the estuary. Mumma and sister Margaret and Leander, Mumma's dog, are all going with him. Simon and me are being taken by Uncle Bill, Captain Owen and his son HD (Horrid David) in their grey dory, *The Joanna*. Horrid David says we have to sit very still and not stand up and tip *The Joanna*, or Captain Owen will make us 'walk the plank'. I don't believe him – anyway where is the 'plank'?

At low tide, sandbanks stretch right across from Padstow to Rock. But when the tide comes in, the sandbanks and the whole huge bay get completely covered in deep water and you wouldn't know they were there. We are going to moor the boats on the sand with the anchors when the tide has gone out, and have a picnic.

17

The tide is still going out when we get there, and all round us the sand is smooth and pale – nobody else's footprints. Father sits on his walking stick thing and starts to draw the view, and Uncle Bill and Mumma light a fire to cook sausages and boil a kettle. The rest of us run into what's left of the water to swim. That pig HD comes in after me and tries to push my head under, but I can swim faster than him, so I dog-paddle away very fast, splashing water in his face. When we come out, the picnic is ready: burnt sausages and egg and cress sandwiches, pieces of chocolate and saffron cake for pudding. Father drops my sausage in the sand and I have to wash it in the salty estuary water. I don't think *he* would like a sandy sausage, but all he says is: 'Good heavens, what a fuss! It's just a bit of sand.' After the picnic, we all start building a huge castle. Everybody digs and digs – even Leander, sand flying everywhere – and it grows bigger and bigger until it is taller than Simon and wide enough for several people to stand on. Uncle Bill and HD make it even higher by digging a deep moat round it.

The afternoon goes by, and water begins to creep back across the sand. Mumma and sister Margaret start packing up, loading the boats with the picnic things, wet towels and bathing costumes. HD climbs on to the castle shouting, 'I'm king of the castle! I'm king of the castle!' but we soon push him off and he goes to help his father get *The Joanna* ready to leave.

The tide is coming in fast, and the sandbanks have almost disappeared. Standing on the top of the castle, we are in the middle of a huge sheet of black green water stretching from Rock across to Padstow and out to the sea. Captain Owen and the others get into the dory, pull up their anchor and push off, Leander swimming along behind. Father, red sails flat against the wind, is in *Summer*

Haze tacking towards the sandcastle to pick us up. But he doesn't. He just sails past us laughing and calling out, 'Better start swimming you two…'

I can swim quite well, but not as far as that! He sails past us again, very fast in the wrong direction. The water is right up to the top of the castle, and he is just whizzing off towards Rock. Suppose he doesn't come back and just leaves us here? Simon is holding on to me very tight, and Mumma and the others are miles away already. Little waves are lapping over our feet and it's a long time until Father turns around, and ages before he brings the boat in close enough for us to climb on board.

'That was fun, wasn't it?' he says. 'Bet you thought I wasn't coming back.'

Grandma sleeps in her bell tent outside on the lawn when she comes to stay – so that she can see the stars at night. (She's not afraid of the spiders and ghosts.) Yesterday we went looking for sea coal on the beach, and I found three cowrie shells.

She and Mumma, the Miss Marleys, everyone, even Father, are getting ready for the regatta. It is to be held in the quarry field, and when we walk up the lane from our house, crowds and crowds of people have arrived already. Grandma is there in a tent, with earrings and a scarf over her head – she is the fortune teller. Near her is a lucky dip – that's a bran tub with mystery packages bought by Mumma from Woolworth's. There is a coconut shy, a shove halfpenny table, and a greasy pole stuck out in the mud waiting for the tide so that Padstow boys can scull up the river to try their luck. Father is looking after the coconut shy, Nanny has got a cake on a plate and you have to guess the weight, and Uncle Toby and Jimmy are arranging an 'obstacle race'. Pig nets are pegged to the ground, and when the starter's gun goes off, men are going to have to scramble underneath them to get at some suitcases filled with ladies clothes and hats, dress up in them, and then run back as fast as they can to the starting place. The first one back wins. They look so funny dressed up in skirts and bonnets that everyone laughs and laughs. All the money that people pay is going to the St Issey Silver Band.

I throw a coconut, but it misses and hits Mr Rowe's foot – the farmer who the quarry field belongs to. Father calls me an idiot, and Mr Rowe is jumping around holding his ankle, but he says that I am a 'dear little maid', and it didn't hurt him at all. In the lucky dip I get some pipe cleaners. Nanny says I can give them to Father for Christmas. Simon gets a packet of marbles. (I am not going to give the pipe cleaners to anyone.) The greasy pole is the best. The boys from Padstow and their friends, even Horrid David, try and try to get to the top. Some of them almost do it, but then they start sliding and slipping, everyone is cheering and laughing, and down they go with a terrific splash into the water. (Most of them can swim, I think.) I wish we could have a regatta every day, but we have to go back to London.

In London, all the leaves on the Heath are bright red and gold, and we go out to tea with other children and their nannies. We have to sit up at the table in their day nurseries, and remember to say thank you for every single thing, even if we don't like it. Today we went to the Bliss's. Their nanny has a brown uniform and is very strict and cross. Not like our Fat Nanny.

There is an enormous shiny piano in the Bliss's drawing room. I have never seen a piano before. It makes me think of a huge black mouth, open, with white teeth smiling, all ready to eat you up! They have lovely paintings on the walls. Green and red apples. When we are down in the hall ready to go home, Mr Bliss, who is called Arthur like Father, is standing there laughing and smiling though his moustache. He has a kind face like a big dog and is calling out 'Goodbye! Goodbye children! Had a happy time? Goodbye everyone' in a squeaky friendly voice. And I think *that's* a nice father. I wish Mr Bliss was my father.

Today I go to school, by myself, on a bus. Mumma and Father follow along behind in their car. When I get home, Nanny asks me all about it, but I couldn't remember anything. I don't want to go again.

I have found out that you have to go to school every day except Saturday and Sunday, whether you want to or not.

The lady who works in the florist's next to the Tube station lives round the corner from us. Her mother and sister and sister's baby who's got something wrong with it, all live together in the same house. This morning, when we went in to buy roses, she told Mumma that their old cat had had kittens, and asked would I like to see them? So now we are walking round to Golden Square where she lives. (Mumma calls it a 'two-up-two-downer'.)

I like the flowers and the flower shop, but not the 'two-up-two-downer'. A nasty smell when the front door is opened, and so small that you have to walk off the pavement straight into the kitchen, and sit down at the table at once. Worst of all there is the baby, popping eyes and a huge bulging head on a tiny little body standing up in a cot in the corner, rattling the bars like an animal at the zoo. (That's where the smell is coming from.) I try not to look, but my head keeps pulling round – and I have seen now, I can't un-see? The kittens are better. Two soft little furry creatures curled up together in a basket with their mother by the stove. She wants to know whether I'd like to take one home, but Mumma says no, Leander – our dog – would gobble him up as soon as look at him.

'What's the matter with the baby?' I ask Mumma on the way home.

'Born like that, poor little thing,' she says. 'How do they manage without a bathroom? You are a lucky girl to be so healthy and strong.'

Woolworth's is my favourite shop – because you can get so much for sixpence, my pocket money each week. Today I buy a sherbet stick for a penny-halfpenny, and a model of a little dog like the one on the 'His Master's Voice' label, and I've got a penny over. After Woolworth's we go to Grove Lodge to ask about Grandma's friend, Mr Galsworthy. He is ill in bed. Minnie, the maid in the brown dress and white hat with a frill round it, opens the door. When Mumma asks how he is, she says: 'Not very well at all, madam, I'm afraid...the poor gentleman.' She has tears trickling down her face under her spectacles! We go home to tea, and in the hall, Mumma whispers to Father, 'JG is dying.' Father says, 'Poor old boy.' But I don't think he is sad like Mumma.

It is winter, and today we got a letter from Father in Switzerland, with drawings of him skiing. He has drawn going up – in a box called a ski-lift hanging from a long wire – and coming down, whizzing down on his skis. I think he is quite good at this. We go for our walk on the Heath with Nanny, along the Spaniards Road and then down to the Vale of Health. Near the sheep pound, the shepherd man is working with his black and white collie, the sheep crowded together in a bunch not knowing which way to go. The Vale of Health pond is frozen and there are some policemen there. Nanny says some children didn't read the notice, and were skating and fell through the ice.

After that we walk past a dogfight. A white bull terrier has grabbed a little brown dog in its mouth and is whirling it round growling and snarling. People are shouting and a lady is screaming. Some park keepers come with sticks and start hitting the dogs, but the bull terrier doesn't let go. Then two men get buckets of freezing water from the pond and throw it over the bull terrier. I don't know what happened next, because Nanny says 'Time for tea!' and we go home. I wish I could go skiing.

We come back early from our walk today because the fog is so bad. A 'pea-souper', greyish yellow, like very thick smoke, creeping into the house smelling of soot and wet coal. Nanny says fog is bad for her, and makes a funny wheezing noise in her bosom. But I like it because it is exciting to see the soft fuzzy lights of cars creeping along in the grey, and being able to hear people but not see them in the street. If I let go of the pram handle, she says I might get lost on the Heath and never be found again. She's joking, I think. We have toasted teacakes, shrimp paste sandwiches and chocolate biscuits for tea, and she tells me a story about a princess who pricks her finger and sleeps for a hundred years, until she's woken with a kiss from a handsome prince. I wanted to know what happened then but she didn't know. I thought a lot about the handsome prince when I was going to sleep. He would be the kindest person in the world, I think.

1933–4

I am visiting Fat Nanny – except it isn't her. She is called Mrs Tanner now. I don't know who this new different person is, in a nasty brick house with a pram in the yard. She is not wearing her lovely veil and pale blue dress or starched apron, and there's a man in braces and no collar sitting reading a newspaper. Mumma says he is Mr Tanner, and I start crying because I want my nanny back like she used to be.

Now that Nanny is Mrs Tanner, I sleep in the sewing room near the front door. Today, the sewing lady Mrs Duck-Duck is visiting us, and the table is covered with piles of clothes and mending. If I am good and don't chatter, she lets me turn the handle of the sewing machine. Her name is Mrs Duck-Duck because she calls everyone 'ducky'. She is letting down the hem of my school dress and then she is going to mend the sheets. I am showing her how I can balance on the fender, when I fall and put my hand on the red coals burning in the fire. I cry and cry – roar – because it hurts so much. Mumma puts a bandage on it, but it doesn't make any difference, it still hurts. I don't want to go to dancing class this afternoon, but Mumma takes me all the same. She says I will feel better if I am a brave girl. It's not true.

I don't know why, I am not tired but when I am not at school I have to rest after lunch. My bedroom now – the same as the sewing room – is on the ground floor, and from the window I can see who is waiting at the front door. Father's other daughter – my grown-up half-sister Margaret – and Uncle Toby were out there today, and see me on my bed practising standing on my head. I am quite good at this. They ask me what I am doing, so I say 'resting!' and they think this is funny and laugh a lot.

I was coming out of the nursery with Simon yesterday, and Mumma was in the hall with our maid Rose standing in front of her with a suitcase. Today, Rose's room between the nursery and the front door is empty and all her things have gone. Mrs Duck-Duck says, 'She's a naughty girl ducky, so she's had to leave.' I ask sister Margaret what she's done, and she just laughs. Uncle Toby calls up to Mumma on the stairs – 'In bed with a *policeman*?' 'Hush,' she says. 'Little pitchers have ears!' She means me. Rose's room looks sad and lonely, and I wonder how a policeman could have fitted into her little bed. It is so small and narrow, and all the policemen I see are giants.

When I go upstairs to say goodnight to Father, I show him how I can stand on my head when I am resting. He doesn't laugh at all.

The Austrian girl, Sensi, is in Rose's room now. She isn't a maid and she isn't a nanny, I don't know what she is. Perhaps she is a friend? Mumma says Sensi is not a friend but a refugee, and we have to be kind to her. What is a refugee?

I go with Mumma to visit our neighbour next door. People are standing listening to the wireless – someone called Hitler shouting in German. A loud, screeching screaming sound floating out through the open window into the sunshine, spoiling it. Everyone is miserable because of this voice. Sensi says that Hitler is a very bad man, but lots of people in Austria and Germany love him. English people don't like this Hitler.

Sensi is teaching me German, words mostly. This is because there is a German coming to stay in our house, Herr Schmidt Pauli. Sensi says he is a 'delegate', invited to one of Grandma's meetings (book people and writers), but nobody else will have him to stay because he is friends with Hitler. Mumma wants me to come up and say goodnight to him in German while he is staying with us. But I heard Father telling her yesterday that he 'didn't like the idea one little bit', and to 'keep the children in the nursery, away from any damned Germans'. Sensi says that this is because when he was young, Father fought the Germans in a terrible war, so of course he doesn't like them, and he doesn't want one in the house.

Anyway, while I am in the sewing room with Sensi, we see this German person arrive in a taxi with all his luggage, cases and cases of it. He is quite large, no hair and with a round glass in one eye. Before we can open the door we hear Father – he must have been waiting in the hall – shouting up the stairs:

'Marjorie…? Marjorie! Here's your bloody Hun!'

At tea, I ask Sensi if I can say 'Guter nacht bloody Hun' because I keep forgetting all the German names I have to learn. But she says no, just say 'Guter nacht' – which is German for goodnight. So that's what I do, and he gives me a half crown!

Sometimes, we go up to the drawing room and Mumma reads to us. Usually I like this. But today she is reading a terrible story about a child called Harriet being burnt to ashes. Simon loves it, but I have to leave the room because I am a cry-baby. So I go down to Sensi, and she gives me one of her chocolates from the tin with a picture of a castle on it. The castle is in the town in Austria where she used to live.

After lunch, I am going to a place called Kenwood because Father wants to look at a painting which belongs to someone there. Simon was supposed to go with him, but he has earache, so Father is allowing me to come instead. We drive along the Spaniards Road, me sitting in the front – I have to behave very well because I am with Father.

The house is huge, shut up and empty because the people are not there at the moment. He brings a big black key, but when we get there someone in a green baize apron called Jenner opens the door. He's a clock winder apparently.

'Hello Jenner,' Father says. 'How are the clocks? Keeping time all right?'

'Pretty fair, sir,' Jenner replies, and we go in.

It's the largest house I've ever seen, very cold and quiet. There is hardly any furniture, and our footsteps make a noise as we walk from room to room. Father says: 'There is a painting here by one of the greatest artists who ever lived, Marjorie-Ann…Rembrandt. Every now and then I like to come and look at it.'

We walk down a passage into a big room, and on the far wall is a big dark painting of an old man looking out of the picture at us with sad tired eyes. I thought it would be a beautiful lady in silks and satins, perhaps with a lovely

27

little dog or a baby with golden curls on her knee, so I don't know what to say. Why does he like it so much?

Father stands for a long time gazing at the old man. Then he shakes his head and says: 'Unforgettable. How did he do it?'

I look at the painting again and think: with paint and a paintbrush. But I am afraid to say anything. It just seems like a poor ugly old man to me, so after a while I go to the window and look out across the park at the lake. I wait for Father to stop staring at his painting – about an hour? – and then, slowly, we walk back through all the rooms again and, because Jenner is winding the clocks up on the first floor now, lock the side door carefully, and drive home.

When I am in bed and Mumma is saying goodnight, I tell her about the painting, and how I wish it had been a beautiful old-fashioned lady or something like that. She says when I am grown-up probably I will like it better. And when she has gone, and my eyes are shut trying to go to sleep, the poor sad old man's face still floats there, just in front of me. So perhaps Father is right, and I will never forget him.

I am sitting at the dining room table, drawing, and Father comes in.

'What are you doing?' he asks me.

'Drawing something.' He bends over me and looks.

'What is that?'

'A bottle.' He takes my piece of paper, and a wine bottle from the sideboard.

'You must *look* at what you are drawing,' he says. 'Really *look*!' He points his pencil at the bottle. 'You see? The top is round…like this,' and very quickly he draws a beautiful bottle on my piece of paper – small, but exactly like the real one. I will never be able to draw like that.

Today I am in the kitchen helping Cook make jam tarts because Mumma has gone to visit Grandma in hospital. Cook says she will put some of mine on a tray with a cup of tea for Mr Watts – that's Father – and I can come with her when she takes it up to him in his studio. We are walking along the passage with the tray, when we meet Mumma back from visiting Grandma.

'How is she, madam?' Cook asks.

'Not good,' she says. 'Not good at all…oh *Cook*!' – and I think she is going to cry. Then she takes the tray, and walks away up the stairs not looking at us.

Next day, Cook tells me that Grandma has gone to Heaven (she means she has died).

'Your poor ma,' she says. So I draw a picture of a beautiful old-fashioned lady in a garden for Mumma, to cheer her up.

In the High Street, some workmen are putting up orange balloon things on black and white sticks. There are going to be lights as well – red for stop, yellow for wait, and green for go. This has all been invented by Mr Horebelisha, to help cars drive properly. But coming out of Mr White's chemist's shop this afternoon with Mumma, it didn't seem to be helping much, because just by the Belisha beacons two cars had smashed into each other, and there was a policeman, and even someone lying on the ground. Quite exciting.

On Christmas Day, Simon and I are going upstairs for lunch. I have to wear my silk tussore party frock and my dancing slippers. Sister Margaret and Uncle Toby and Jimmy, and lots of people I don't know, are sitting at a long table sparkling with silver and glass. I sit next to Sensi, as I don't like crackers that bang and everybody laughing and making such a noise. The candles on the Christmas tree in the corner are lit, and make everything shine and glisten. (What would happen if it caught fire? Everyone would be burnt to ashes?) It looks beautiful, but I am still frightened – and everybody is laughing such a lot, I don't know why. After a long time, the presents are given out from under the tree and I get a doll who opens and shuts her eyes (she has eyelashes). I am supposed to thank Mumma and Father, but I don't like dolls so I don't know what to do. Sensi whispers 'say thank you to your mummy and daddy' – but I can't.

1935

It is summer time and Mumma is in Cornwall with Simon, and Father is on holiday – in Italy or somewhere. Sensi says we are going to have a new baby soon, and she combs my hair and puts a ribbon in it. I think she is my friend.

Today, Uncle Toby and sister Margaret are taking me and Sensi to Cornwall in the car to see Mumma's new baby. Because it's so far, we have to stop for the night at the house of a family called Pidcock, a funny name. When we arrive, I have to eat scrambled eggs – wet and runny and horrible – so I feel sick. Then Mrs Pidcock says, 'Come upstairs dear' – which makes me wonder, is she going to make me go to bed already? But in her bedroom, all soft green and pale colours like an aquarium, she says, 'I have something very sad to tell you. Your daddy is very ill.' I just look at her, and she goes on, 'Very, very ill.' I say, 'Is he dead?' 'Yes, dear,' and I think about the graveyard and the stones, and what a huge one he will have to have. I say, 'Who is going to earn the money then?' but I can't remember the answer, because then, suddenly, I am sick all over the pale green carpet.

After breakfast the next day, we get in the car and drive to Cornwall again. Days and days. Sister Margaret says Father was in an aeroplane that went into the side of a mountain in a snowstorm, and he is dead – do I understand? Dead. What a pity.

Mumma's face looks different. Red and shiny with lines. She doesn't notice me, and spends a long time hugging sister Margaret and Uncle Toby. I think she is crying. Simon is standing next to her holding on to her dress. Does he know about Father? Sensi comes with us down to the little slate beach near the house to look for tiny crabs. I find five at once, and Simon only has two. So I give him one of mine.

There is a nurse here that I have never seen before who looks after people's babies. Mumma's baby is called Julyan. I go and say hello and make faces at him, but stop because he looks so small and lonely. (He doesn't open his eyes, so he doesn't know I am making faces.).

Mumma is in bed. Sensi says she is having a rest because she is sad, and we must play quietly in the garden. In the afternoon Dr Shirvell comes to see Mumma and the new baby. Before he gets driven away by his chauffeur, he asks to see us.

'And how are we?' he says, looking very hard at us both with his pale blue watery eyes in an old red face. 'I hope you are a comfort to your mother, children? How old are you laddie?'

'Six,' Simon says (actually, he is five years and six months).

'Well, you have to look after your mother now, laddie – and you too, young lady. Make your father proud, eh?' He picks up his black doctor's bag and mutters to Sensi, 'When's the funeral?' Sensi whispers something, but I can't hear what because they walk away towards the gate. Will they put Father in the ground with a stone over him then? I feel sorry for him suddenly, and start crying.

The baby nurse has gone, and we have a new nanny called Klara. She comes from Norway and wears a blue and white striped uniform and a white starched veil on her head. She looks after Simon and Julyan, and me when I am not at school. Sensi has gone away – to America Mumma says – I don't know why. I wish I had said goodbye.

Now that Father is not here any more, his studio has my doll's house and Simon's train set in it and is called the day nursery. Simon has a black Hornby Doublo engine and tender that goes round and round pulling brown and cream Pullman carriages with tiny pink lamps in the windows that light up. It looks quite real. I have a doll's house with electric lights which turn on and off too. Klara is helping me make matchbox furniture for it. She says she likes the doll's house so much because she never had one when she was little – what a lucky girl I am. But I don't really like dolls or their houses; the train is my favourite.

Sister Margaret comes to visit. She is beautiful with a white face, red lips and black fur coat. She says, 'Are you thinking about Daddy a lot?' and looks very sad, so I say: 'Yes, a lot.' 'Poor sweetie,' she says. Actually, I am not thinking about him at all.

Our house is almost at the top of a hill (Holly Hill). If I hang out of the side window of the studio, I can look down at the row of cottages below. Each one has a tin bath hanging on the wall outside, and each little back garden is different from the one next door: a few roses in one, mostly grass and nettles in the next, stacked-up planks, old mattresses and builder's rubbish in the next, rusting iron pieces in another. But one of them is completely black – like Mr Kippin, the sweep who lives there; and like his bags of black soot and brushes on the black handcart we see him pushing through the street, and which he keeps in his back garden down there.

The children who live in the cottages sometimes play out on the pavement; skipping games and hopscotch. Klara calls them the 'poor little heathens'. We are not allowed to go out and play on the pavement, but we watch them from the sewing room. They are mostly rather small, and have black broken teeth or no teeth at all. Klara says that's because they don't use toothbrushes or go to the dentist like we do. The boy who brings up the order from Sainsbury's on a bicycle lives in the end cottage. His teeth are all right, but I don't know his name.

Father's big black grandfather clock is still up in the studio standing in its corner. Every now and then, you hear the machinery inside whirring and then it chimes whatever time it is, and tells you whether its Saturday or Monday or Friday and things like that – I am not sure how. It has a big flat silvery clock sort of face with hands that go round very slowly. Above that is a polished smiling sun, with wiggly polished flames arranged in a circle. Every few days Klara winds the weights up to the top with a special handle, and then they start slowly unwinding down again. That's how it keeps going.

33

Today Simon opened the little door in the case and we watched the pendulum swinging from side to side ticking and tocking, the heavy weights on their chains hanging there and moving so slowly you don't notice.

'If somebody dropped those weights out of the window, they would bounce back,' Simon says.

'No they wouldn't, they're too heavy!'

'We could catch them!'

'They would go bashing through to the other side of the world…'

'Through to China?'

The weights are almost too heavy to lift, but we do it in the end and Simon pulls up the sash. We hang out of the window and it is a long way to the ground, but there is nobody down there. Simon drops his weight. Then I let go of mine.

Nothing much happens except we hear two loud clanging sort of bangs and then a rumble. The weights don't break or anything, just roll into the gutter.

'Oh,' Simon says – he's disappointed, but I'm older than him and actually I knew they wouldn't bounce.

Klara is in the bathroom with Julyan, so we run down to the front hall and out into the street as quickly as we can (probably she'd be cross about dropping things out of the window). The weights look more or less the same, but the pavement has got two long deep cracks in the paving stones now. Nobody will ever guess how they got there!

We saw some of the little Heathens today, out with their fat wheezing mother near the bathhouse in Flask Walk and Klara stopped to 'have a chat'. Simon and me – and Julyan asleep in the pram – all have to wait and not interrupt while they talk. The other pram is full of bundles of washing, and a baby with its mouth open and yellow stuff dribbling out of its nose. Quite disgusting.

'Bathhouse is it today Mrs Hoskins?' Klara asks, all friendly.

'Always the same with kiddies...' the fat lady shakes her head.

'How's the little one?' Klara bends over the baby.

'Cough, cough, cough all night.'

'I have some linctus, blackcurrant, left over from last winter if you like?' Klara says.

Don't give her that, I think, it's horrible, but I don't say anything because I am right up close looking at Mrs Hoskins's legs. She is wearing bedroom slippers and no stockings and they are not like ordinary legs at all, but very fat and white, shiny, with thick blue veins bunched up under the skin like worms. Her petticoat is sort of hanging down, so I can't see very far – whether her legs are like that all the way up, I mean.

'It's cough, cough, cough all night,' she says again. Then I stop listening because a dray from the brewery with four big bay horses has got stuck behind a removal van in the narrow bit going up to Back Lane, and the two drivers have jumped down into the road and are shouting at each other. I watch, hoping there will be a fight, but a policeman comes along and starts writing in his notebook.

'Wake up, Marjorie-Ann...we are going now,' Klara says.

'Why is she taking her washing to the bathhouse?'

'Some people don't have bathrooms and places to wash their clothes.'

'Why are her legs like that and why are we not allowed to talk to them and you are?'

'Too many questions. Hold on to the pram, we are crossing the road.'

35

Two doors away from us is the Catholic church. We don't like Catholics, especially the old priest we sometimes see in the yard at the back of our house, Father George. He wears a sort of black frock and shouts at us, and Mumma calls him a disagreeable old toad. But she likes my friend Moira Malone, although she is a Catholic.

The Malones live at the bottom of the hill, and I run down to play there quite often. We get into the hollow tree near the fence at the end of their garden, and climb up inside and drop twigs and things on people in the street below. Her brother Tony (Tony Maloney) has a water pistol, and sometimes we hide in the tree and fire water at people on the pavement underneath. They think it's raining!

Mumma often says bad things about Catholics. One day when she is in a good mood, I ask her why, and she says 'because of the Fenians'. I don't know who they are, but then she tells me a story. Once when she was a little girl, she and her brothers saw some brown paper parcels waiting in their father's surgery; he was a doctor, and they were not allowed in that part of the house. But her brothers had a look, and inside there were some guns. They closed up the parcels quickly, and didn't say anything. Later, when they came back, the parcels had gone.

'It was my father, you see,' she says. 'He was an Ulsterman, smuggling guns against the Fenians!' She looks all excited when she says this, but I still don't know who they are or why she doesn't like Catholics.

Klara wears a blue-and-white-striped dress, white apron, and a stiff shiny white collar and belt: keeps her all together she says. Best of all is her white starched veil which blows out behind her like a sail. I love it when we go out on the Heath with her and the pram, because she looks so grand and beautiful and she is our special nanny. Usually, we walk to a place on the Heath where there is a sandy path good for digging, and a grass paddock surrounded by trees and bushes where we can run about or ride our fairy cycles. We have to keep out of the way of any park keepers, as you are only supposed to ride bicycles on the cycle track. The keepers – we call them 'Parkers' – walk round the Heath day and night keeping order; picking up any rubbish they see on the end of their long pointed stabber things, and shouting at people if they do something wrong.

The nannies – blue, green, mauve, pink – sit on the wooden benches by the path and knit, and their children play in the sand or the long grass nearby. The Farqharson nanny wears a mauve dress and white collar and belt, but no apron. The Garnet nanny, who is fat and very old with loops of grey hair on either side of her face, wears a white uniform and veil and even her stockings are white. Some have twins to look after, and they have an especially large double-hooded twin pram big enough for a baby at either end. (Twins don't make any difference to what uniforms they wear.) The Blisses have a Norland nanny and she always wears brown – brown coat, brown dress and a little round brown hat. Norlands are terribly strict, and I think the Bliss children have to curtsey to their mother when they say goodnight.

Usually the babies sleep or sit in their prams and we play and dig in the sand, or the bigger boys try to catch the wasps that go in and out of their little holes all along the path. Sometimes we just stay with Klara, or perhaps climb into one of the trees near the paddock. As long as we don't go too far away, the nannies talk to each other and knit, and don't take much notice of exactly what we are doing.

A few days ago, one of the Garnet boys thought of a new game – 'lover baiting'. You find some lovers a little distance away lying kissing and cuddling in the long grass, and, very quietly, creep towards them on your tummy until you are almost on top of them. At the last moment, you suddenly jump up making a 'holla, holla' Red Indian sort of noise and rush round them in a circle, shrieking and screaming and waving your arms.

Today we were playing this game, but it went wrong. The man of the couple got up suddenly and chased us. We rushed back to the bench, but he came after us and stood and shouted and yelled furiously at all the nannies. Klara stood up – she is quite tall and big – and said, 'That's enough! And please mind your language in front of children, sir,' but it didn't make any difference – he just went on and on. Klara was very stern and angry with us when we told her about the game. She said we would be sent to bed early without any tea if we ever did anything like that again. Then we had to pack up and walk home holding on to the pram all the way and we were not allowed to talk as a punishment. Julyan is still too little to play any games, so she is not cross with him.

1936

We are staying in a cottage near the water with Miss Mavis, Mumma's friend. She has a funny hairstyle: two grey plaits on either side of her head wound up into a sort of tuft like feathers. Her two big teeth in the front stick out, and she rides a motorbike. Sometimes she gives us rides in the sidecar up and down the village street.

Itchenor, where we are staying, is where the river Itchen goes out to the sea. At the end of the street, lots of boats are moored off the Hard, including Mumma's little dinghy *Curlew* and the Pidcock's barge, *The Dolphin*. At high tide the boats float, but when the tide goes out they sink down on the mud (like in Cornwall, but we don't go there any more). The water is salty and you can sail out past Hayling Island as far as the sea, if you want. And if anybody needs to get across the river, old Captain Haynes will row you to the Bosham side for a shilling. He was a pirate when he was young and wears a red handkerchief round his neck, a flat yachting cap and little gold rings in his ears. If you are playing about in one of the empty dinghies moored on the Hard, you have to watch he doesn't come up behind you and thump down his length of knotted rope with a sudden bang to give you a fright.

This morning we are messing about in Miss Mavis's little dinghy and looking at the big yachts moored out in deep water. I am at the tiller, and Simon is rowing. If the tarpaulins over the hatches on some of the bigger yachts are battened down and there's nobody about, we tie up the dinghy, climb on board and walk around to have a look. We are rowing past one of the biggest yachts of all, *The Bounty*, when somebody on board, a sailor, calls to us and says we can come up if we like and he'll show us the boat. So we climb up the ladder, and Simon is shown all the brass fittings, the new coils of rope, teak hatches, electric winches and, best of all, the engine (Simon loves engines). We stay looking at this for a long time.

The sailor is…I don't know, I don't like him. He is drinking out of a brown bottle – beer, I think – and keeps staring at me. He puts his hand on my neck under my hair at the back and tries to tickle me, but I wriggle away.

'Let's go, shall we?' I say. But Simon wants to go on looking at the engine, so we stay. The sailor is smiling a lot, too much somehow, and he keeps on staring at me.

'Pretty little girl,' he says. 'How old are you then?' I don't answer and after a while he climbs down the companionway into the saloon cabin below. I want to get back in the dinghy, but Simon is still looking at the engine. Then the sailor calls up to me to come down – he has something he wants to show me. I look down the companionway and see him lying on a bunk drinking out of his brown bottle with his trousers undone, his great big winkle poking out.

'Come on down,' he calls again, 'I won't hurt you… I've got something for you here,' and suddenly everything is wrong and horrible, and I want to get off the boat as quickly as possible.

'We've got to go!' I say. 'Simon!' And I start climbing down the ladder. 'Come on!'

'Why? I don't want to…what's the matter, where are you going?'

'Come *on*!'

'Wait…I am coming. Why?'

I untie the mooring ropes and am in the dinghy with the oars in the rowlocks in a flash, and as soon as Simon's feet touch the bottom boards I start rowing back to the Hard as fast as I can.

'What's happened? Why do we have to go?' Simon asks again.

I can't explain. I keep seeing the sailor's smiling face and that look, and a terrible feeling like a nightmare comes over me. We moor the dinghy, and walk up to Miss Mavis's cottage. As soon as Mumma sees me, she says 'What's the matter?' and I burst into tears, I don't know why.

Next day, when we are walking to the bakery to get our bread, we meet the sailor in the high street.

'It's him, it's him,' I mutter, trying to hide.

'Ah! So it's *you*!' Mumma says to him in an extremely fierce voice, pulling me out from behind her skirt. 'What's your name? You should be ashamed of yourself! What do you mean by frightening my daughter yesterday? You can apologise to her now...well? Go on, I am waiting...' she says very loudly and fiercer than ever. 'Apologise! Or I shall report you to *The Bounty*'s owner. Do you hear me?'

He mumbles something about it just being a bit of fun, and that he's sorry, he didn't mean any harm, and then walks away looking at the ground. After that, although I sometimes think about him, I am not as frightened as I was.

Today, Granny is coming to London and we are having tea with her at the Strand Palace Hotel. She is old and extremely tall, with a loud voice. Father's mother. She wears a high-necked long black gown and coat, a black satin squashed sort of hat with a veil hanging down over her face. At tea, when she wants to eat something, she lifts up the veil and pins it to her hat with a long pearled hat pin. Underneath the hat, her hair is piled up in little round grey puffs like meringue. Long chains of beads hang down from her neck, and a ribbon with some silver-framed spectacles attached, which she snaps open to look at you. She always wears gloves – even when she is eating ice cream – and always books a table near the orchestra so that Julyan can watch the violins playing.

The tables in the tea room of the Strand Palace Hotel are covered by white tablecloths as stiff as cardboard with napkins folded into fans. The cups and plates have gold rims and handles, and we eat our cakes and sandwiches with large silver knives and forks. Fizzy lemonade comes in thin fluted glasses with a straw. The order is taken by a tall man in evening dress, and served by a 'Nippy' – a pretty girl in a black dress and apron and a sort of little white lace frill on her head.

Granny likes to tell us stories about when she was in India – she married a young army captain at only eighteen and sailed out there to join him.

'There I was, only married a month, went into my bedroom and lo and behold, on the floor was the poor maid in the coils of a twelve-foot boa constrictor...blue in the face and quite, quite dead the poor soul. Suffocated!'

Or, 'I opened the drawer and there was the most poisonous snake in all India, coiled up amongst my stockings! One bite from him and that was the end, my dears.'

Simon's favourite stories are about the faithful manservant, Anil, who saved her life, not once but many times.

'I was about to put on my boots to accompany my husband on a tiger hunt, but in the nick of time Anil leaped forward to shake the boots first. Out dropped not one, but two scorpions!'

Or, 'I was following my husband through the forest on a mule when, a few paces ahead, Anil spotted a sixteen-foot python uncoiling from the tree above my head, and with one shot killed it instantly!'

She had a terribly dangerous and exciting life in India but it didn't last long, as her gallant army husband died of yellow fever, and she had to come home with her poor fatherless little boy (Father) and marry someone else.

When we get back from having cucumber sandwiches, anchovy paste toasts, strawberry trifle, and ice cream with Granny, not only are we full up to our chins, but the whole house is suddenly and frighteningly dangerous! Snakes and scorpions lurk in every corner – especially under and at the bottom of our beds at bedtime.

I could listen to Granny forever, but Mumma is embarrassed by her loud voice, and the looks people give her, especially when she is talking about Hitler.

'Mr Hitler is a good thing, Marjorie. A bit of discipline never hurt anybody. You are soft, dear.'

We are going to the Wilkinsons for Christmas dinner. Mr Norman Wilkinson paints seascapes – ships and raging storms at sea. He and Father were best friends, and he has an artist wife who paints flowers. They live in a big house near Kenwood and the whole of the downstairs floor has been made into a very large studio smelling of turpentine and paint. Paintings are stacked up against the walls, and usually the one he is working on is up on an easel. Today I am looking at an enormous painting of some battle or other, lots of dark grey battleships in a choppy sea off Dover. He asks me what I think of it, so I say I don't like it very much, because the paint is so thick. (Mumma is frowning, and whispers that I shouldn't have said anything. But he did ask me…)

After Christmas, we are going to France, skiing in a place called the French Alps, Haute-Savoie! Just Mumma and me and Simon. Julyan will stay with Klara. We are going by train and then boat, and staying the night in Paris on the way.

1937

Paris has a different smell from London, and the noises are different too. French people speak French, of course, but very fast and loud, as if they are having an argument all the time. Mumma understands French, but I don't know what they are talking about. The porters and working men wear wooden shoes – clogs that clack, clack, clack on the pavement as they clop along – blue overalls or blouses, and flat black hats called berets.

Our hotel is in a small village high up in the mountains. Everything is covered in deep, deep snow, and Simon and I go skiing every day. We have a guide called Francois who teaches us. The house where he lives has long icicles hanging down from the snow-covered roof, and stone steps covered in snow up the outside to where the family live. Below them on the ground floor are their cows brought in for the winter. And if you peep through a crack in the living room floor, underneath you can see their backs, hear them chewing their hay and stamping their feet.

Today we went with Mumma to look at a waterfall which has frozen almost solid – just a few drops of water tinkling inside. When the sun shines, the crusted ice melts a little at the edges and flashes like a million diamonds. Simon climbed up and broke a bit off and put it in his pocket. But then it melted and made his skiing trousers wet.

At the hotel, we have our meals in the dining room with all the other guests. At the next table there is a young couple, honeymooners. All through meals they sit looking into each other's eyes, and slipping their wedding rings backwards and forwards on each other's fingers. Mumma says it's because they are 'so much in love', but I think they look silly. One of the other guests, Mr Roberts, who is on a skiing holiday like us, sometimes comes and sits at our table and laughs and talks to Mumma. He tries to be jokey with us, but Simon won't talk to him, and I don't either. He is too friendly with Mumma, so we always behave as badly as possible when he's there, horrid man.

Mumma says that usually children can ski almost at once. And it's true. Soon, Simon and I are zooming up and down the mountain faster than all the grown-ups. Most of them can hardly ski at all, and they look so funny when they fall over in the snow.

I wish we could stay here forever, but of course we can't. And today we have to leave. It is night, and we are not stopping in Paris this time. In the train we have to sleep in the luggage rack!

Moira Malone and I are playing upstairs in the studio (we still call it that). She is standing by one of the windows looking out at the flat roof of the Catholic church.

'I dare you to get out of here and walk across the roof!' she says. 'Bet you won't.'

Outside the line of windows, there is a parapet with a little wall to stop you falling off, and it's quite easy. Klara is downstairs, so I open the window and climb out. Very soon we are out on the hot grey roof of the church. We walk around for a bit – you can see for miles, right across London – and then Moira finds a round porthole and opens it. In the dark church far down below us, picked out by a bright ray of sunshine, is the altar and brass rail, and in front of it, flowers.

'I dare you to spit on the altar,' she whispers. 'Go on…I dare you!' So I lean over and, after a minute, spit as hard as I can.

'Now you'll go to hell,' Moira says.

'No I won't…it was your idea.'

'Fiery burning hell,' Moira says, 'you'll burn *forever*!'

I think about when I put my hand on the fire when I was little. It can't be true, can it?

We go back across the roof to the edge of the parapet, and I walk along carefully and climb back through the window. When I turn round, Moira says she is frightened, and can't move. So I go and find Klara. She is very cross, and talks to Moira out of the window – telling her to come in at once. But she starts crying, and in the end Klara goes and gets the milkman, who is standing in the road far below with his horse and some of the little Heathens, watching, and she asks him to come up and help Moira. They get her in at last, and she is taken home. I have to go and sit in the sewing room, now my bedroom, by myself, until Mumma comes, which is not for a long time. I tell her about Moira and the dare, about spitting and that it wasn't my idea, and…is there really a fiery burning hell?

She doesn't answer, just looks half cross and half sad like she usually does. After a while she says, 'I'll have to speak to Mrs Malone if Moira is going to fill you up with her wretched Catholic nonsense.' I start crying because, in spite of what's happened, Moira is still my best friend. 'I just don't want you going anywhere near that *church*! You are to keep right away from now on…do you understand?' Her voice is quite loud and angry. Silence for a long time and then, 'And getting out of the window like that…why are you so naughty, Marjorie-Ann?' So I know that she didn't believe me when I said it was Moira's idea.

The next time I am up in the studio, bars have been fixed over the lower half of all the windows.

We are down in the yard at the back of Holly Place and Simon and Klara are making a boat…well, a sailing raft.

It is really a plank, pointed at one end with a mast and a square sort of sail made from a piece of sheet. When Klara and he first took it up to the Whitestone Pond – where people sail their model yachts on Sunday mornings – it was top-heavy and turned upside down in the water. But now it has two broomsticks sticking out on either side with empty bottles full of air tied on the ends – Simon calls them 'outriggers'. He says it will keep its balance now. We launch it again today, and this time the raft-boat stays upright! The wind fills the sail and blows it across to the other side of the pond, collecting several model sailing yachts on the way and pushing them along as well. Quite good. The owners of the yachts aren't too pleased, but Klara takes off her shoes and stockings, pulls up her skirt and goes into the pond to untangle them, and then it is all right.

Before we go home, I want to have a ride on one of the donkeys who are always waiting in a bunch on that side of the pond, but Klara says she doesn't have enough money. Then the Eldorado man comes by on his tricycle thing shouting '*El-dor-A-do! Ice cream, buy my ice cream!*' and luckily she has enough for that. (I think she wants one herself.) While we are eating them, we watch the Punch and Judy show with the other children standing together on the corner. It's always the same story: Punch is squeaking and dancing about hitting Judy and the policeman and even his poor baby. The policeman and a hangman try and catch him, but he bashes them as well. Then suddenly, the crocodile comes up behind him and he doesn't notice – even though all the children start shouting and yelling: 'Crocodile! Behind you! *Crocodile!*'

'Where? Where?' Punch squeaks, looking in the wrong direction. The crocodile is snapping his mouth open and shut, and the children are laughing and pointing.

47

'Behind you!'

Punch gets bitten and bitten and is hit on the head with the policeman's truncheon – clack, bang, wallop – but it can't be too bad, because he's always back with the Punch and Judy man the next Sunday. And then you can see it all again.

Mumma is having French lessons – I don't know why because she can speak French already. Monsieur Reynard, she calls him Paul, comes to the house quite often to give them to her. I don't like him much and when I come into the drawing room and see him on the sofa laughing and talking to Mumma and not noticing me, suddenly I hate him.

'Say good afternoon to Monsieur Reynard, Marjorie-Ann,' Mumma says, but I don't say anything. Just stare at him. 'Marjorie-Ann?'

'I don't want to!'

'If you can't behave properly and be polite, leave the room please,' Mumma says very sternly. As I walk towards the door, I can feel their four eyes boring into my back, so I bang the door.

Later on Mumma gives me a lecture about being polite to friends and people who come to the house, and I hate Monsieur Reynard even more.

I go for a walk with Mumma today, alone – I mean without Simon or anybody. We walk along the cycle track to the hockey field and sit down on the bench there. The birds are singing and the grass looks alive it is so green. Mumma says: 'Soon, you are going to another school, Marjorie-

Ann…in the country. You will be staying there, with lots of other little girls. New friends…'

'Staying?' The hockey field, grass, trees all round us, look quite different suddenly. Unfamiliar, frightening. Mumma is looking at me, smiling.

'You'll love it, darling.'

'Stay? You mean sleep there? By myself?'

'Yes, everyone does. It's a boarding school. Lots of nice little girls like you…'

'I don't want to.'

'You don't know that yet. Just try it…then if you don't like it you can come home. Everybody comes home for holidays anyway.'

'I want to stay here.'

'You'll love it.' I start crying because it's hopeless – she has made up her mind. 'Don't be such a cry-baby,' Mumma says. 'Lots of things to do, new friends? I want you to give it a try. You're going to love it… promise!'

I have to have all sorts of new clothes for boarding school, and Mrs Duck-Duck has come to sew name tapes on everything, alter the new school winter coat, take up the hem of the navy blue tunic and two silk tussore Sunday dresses, make the laundry bags and shoe bags with my name on them. I have two dozen handkerchiefs and eight pairs of new shoes – brown indoor with a button at the side, two pairs of outdoor lace-ups, galoshes, black gym shoes, shiny dancing pumps. Mrs Duck-Duck has to ink my name in all of them with a special black marking pen. As well as all that, I have to have a blazer with a badge on the top pocket, two cardigans, six pairs of black lisle stockings and two pairs of liberty bodices to hold them up; knickers, vests, shirts, a navy blue hat with a ribbon round it and a school scarf. It all goes into a large brown shiny trunk brought down from Father's dressing room.

'Are you looking forward to your new school ducky?' asks Mrs Duck-Duck, and I start crying again.

The day comes when I actually have to get ready to go to boarding school. Uncle Toby is going to take me in his car. I sit on the trunk in the hall dressed in my new uniform, feeling sick. If only I could be really ill, or die? Or perhaps I could go downstairs and hide under the stairs in the coal hole? But I know they'd find me, and Mumma would be terribly angry if all my new clothes were black.

In the car, Uncle Toby talks to me and tells me stories to cheer me up, but I look out of the window most of the way. I don't know what else to do. We drive through some big gates and up a long, long drive to the school; that's so the children can't run away too easily, I suppose. Uncle Toby rings the bell and a lady comes into the hall – Miss Brown-Douglas. She has black hair cut into a fringe, flat curls stuck to the side of her face, small black dangling earrings. Although she is smiling, she has a bad face. Uncle Toby says: 'Time to say goodbye, chaps…I'll leave you in the capable hands of Miss Brown-Douglas then…' and with a lot of smiling and shaking hands, off he goes.

'Now Marjorie,' Bad Face says, 'we'll go upstairs and I'll show you which dormitory you are in. Take your suitcase, the trunk can come up later.' I turn to start up the wide shining oak stairs behind us, but she says: 'Not these stairs – this is the staff staircase. You go up the back stairs…over there.' She points. 'I'll see you at the top.'

The suitcase is very heavy but I haul it up. When I get to the top she is waiting, and I say, 'I need a wee…please.'

'I *beg* your pardon?'

'The lavatory.'

She says, '*Please, Miss Brown-Douglas, I need to be excused.*'

'Yes…please, Miss Brown-Douglas…' I am going to do it in my knickers if I don't get there soon.

She smiles her bad-face smile and says: 'We have a lot of new things to learn, don't we? This way.'

I hate, *hate*, this place. There are so many stupid rules I feel I am tied up with hundreds of different bits of string. If we want to talk to a teacher we must put up a hand first. We must walk everywhere and not run, not jump the bottom step or whistle or talk in the passages. We even have to sit in a special way, knees together, back straight. I still can't do my tie knot up very well, and the hateful suspender things which hold up my stockings rub the soft part of my legs and make them sore. My hair has to be tied back because it is so untidy, and quite often I am talking when I should be quiet. Big girls called prefects watch us to see when we have done something wrong, and then they give us a 'mark' – five 'marks' and we have to go to Miss Gillespie. She is the junior school head, and looks like a horrible scrawny old turkey with tortoise-shell spectacles on the end of her beak. I haven't been sent to her yet. Lessons go on all day until 'games' (that and art are the only lessons I like, and music). In the evening there is homework. On Sundays before church, there is learning the 'collect' – a different one every week. (What *is* a collect?) After tea, we sit in the common room and have to write letters home. You are not allowed to say 'please come and take me away from this horrible place, I hate it here' – so I can never think of anything. It takes ages, and then the spelling mistakes are corrected and it has to be copied out again. On Saturday and Sunday afternoons we go for a walk, two by two along the macadam road for miles. I don't have a friend so I have to walk with Isobel, who nobody likes. The worst is in bed at night. I sleep in a dormitory with five other girls, whispering and giggling, farting, sometimes crying. Sob, sob. A bell goes in the morning for us to get up, and another one at night when we are supposed to stop talking. We are not allowed to talk after it has rung, and Matron stands outside dormitory doors to try and catch us. Then we get sent to Miss Gillespie. I would like to cut Matron up in very small pieces, and throw them out of the window – no, burn them. And burn down the whole school, too.

I have a diary in my stocking drawer and I cross off the days, one by one. Until the holidays, there are fifty-three days and ten hours, five minutes left, not counting today and the last day. And after that, years. Years and years…

II
1939–1941
Cornwall

Summer holidays with the Boswell family, and we are all staying at Treago Farm near Crantock Beach: lots of cats begging for food and some piglets that race about the yard squealing. Ma and I are in the sea – jumping over waves and surfing in on the big ones – when the Boswell mother, Ma's friend Jean, comes running towards us across the beach and into the water. She is shouting: 'It's war, Marjorie! War!'

Tonight, the two families make a bonfire on the beach, put potatoes in the ashes and boil a kettle for tea. It gets very late, and we play about on the beach with the Boswell children while the other parents and Ma are gathered round the fire wrapped in blankets, talking. Sometimes their mother, or ours, is in tears. When I ask why, Ma says it's because in a war a lot of people you love get killed. But the only thing I can think about is that I am not going back to boarding school. So I run into the sea in the dark and swim quite a long way along the silver track in the water made by the moon.

When I come back to the bonfire in my towel, the farmer from Treago is there, saying he doesn't think we ought to have a bonfire because it's a war now, and the Germans might see the light from the flames and come and bomb the beach and the farm.

Ma has decided that it is better if we don't go back to London at all, but stay on in Cornwall in her wooden bungalow, twelve miles up the coast. She is going to find a

day school here for us to go to, or she will teach us herself
– I didn't know you were allowed to do that? – and we'll
manage somehow or other. *I am not going back to boarding
school!* I am so happy, but is it really true?

Yes, it is. We have moved into the bungalow, and are
living here properly. Uncle Toby brought some of our
things from London in his car, and the rest is being stored
in his house in St John's Wood. Ma says she has decided
definitely to teach us herself at home, but she hasn't started
yet. Uncle Toby is going to join the army.

I love it here. We go swimming every day, and there is
no school! Today I climb far out over the rocks at Booby's,
and then dive into a deep pool where the tide is swelling
in and out gently as if the sea is rocking a cradle. Fringes
of orange and pink weed sway with the tide, and the water
is like green glass and so clear I can see a crab walking
sideways across the sand at the bottom. I stay here treading
water for a long time.

Some stupid person has started an Evacuee School in a hotel
across the cliffs in the bay next to ours, so we have to go
to school after all. Not boarding, though. All the children
who are down here with their mothers – the fathers are in
London, or away somewhere fighting – collect outside our
gate after breakfast, and we walk across the cliffs to lessons.
(Not Julyan – he's still too little, lucky thing.)

There are only two teachers: Miss Tearle who looks
like a giraffe and Miss Negus who is more of a hedgehog.
The colonel, who lives with them, takes them shopping
in his battered old Sunbeam Talbot. When we are in St
Merryn one day, Grace Hawkey, who helps her dad at the
garage, tells us that the two teachers and the colonel all
sleep together in one big bed: some boys from the village

peeped through a crack in the curtains one night and saw them. Ma says, 'Grace, you shouldn't spread rumours. It's bad for the war effort.'

Ma had this bungalow built when she was young. It has got six small rooms and is made of wood. The walls are very thin, and if someone is weeing in the lavatory you can hear them in the sitting room. Ma drew out the plan on the back of an envelope and forgot to put in a front door. So you come in through the kitchen or the French windows of the little sitting room. When there is a storm – which happens quite often – the wind roars down the chimney and blows smoke back into the room, the rain slapping against the windows, which makes them leak. And the creaking groaning wood makes the bungalow sound like a ship at sea. Roofs often blow right off in Cornwall!

Ma wants to dig up part of the garden to grow vegetables, and me and Simon have to help (even though we don't like vegetables). We are taking off the turf that grows on top of a big bit of lawn, and then digging over the sand underneath. Our neighbour, Mrs Hainselin (we call her the Dragon), on the way up to the shop with her yappy little terrier, looks over the wall. She says it's too sandy and nothing will grow and even if it does it will be eaten by rabbits.

'Our dog will chase the rabbits,' Ma says. When the Dragon has gone, I say, 'But we haven't got a dog?' 'We'll get one,' Ma says.

Freathy Tippet comes to help us get the top layer of turf off, and then we all dig and dig the sandy soil beneath until we are red in the face. Next he plants seeds and we water them in. We have to carry the water in buckets, one after the other, which is hard work. The Dragon looks over the wall again – red veins like a fire all over her face, and a top heavy prow sticking out in front. She talks with a lit cigarette jabbing up and down in her mouth. 'Why don't you – jab – use a hose – jab jab – for your watering – jab jab jab?' she says, blowing clouds of smoke out of her awful red nose as she watches us. (Of course we don't have a hose and nor does Freathy.)

The next day, we have to dig out a pit for the rubbish – they don't have dustmen down here. It has to be deep and wide. When it is filled up and brimming with rubbish, earth, or in our case sand, is put on top to stop the rats (it doesn't stop them), and we start again somewhere else. Luckily it is a big garden, so there is plenty of room. Simon and Roland and the other boys have rat hunts. Rats jump sideways when they are chased.

It is getting dark when we walk back from school now. Today, I tell the others to go on home and climb down the cliff. The moon is very bright, huge, and I take off my clothes and walk into the silver water and swim. It is very quiet and calm, just the soft swish and gurgle of the sea, like some huge animal breathing all around me. I swim out into the next cove and back again, and then climb up the cliff to the grass above. Ma is furious, yelling at me when I arrive home, not because I am late but because I had gone swimming alone. She says it is dangerous, but I always feel so safe in the sea.

Major Selby-Smith's springer spaniel has had puppies, and I am to have one for Christmas. What shall I call it?

At Christmas, Uncle Toby comes to spend three days leave with us and say goodbye. He has joined the army, and is a captain. He looks very smart and handsome in his new uniform, but Ma is sad. I suppose she thinks he will be killed? Even though Simon is three years younger than me, Uncle Toby tells him that he is the man of the family now and has to look after us. After he's gone, Simon says that the war is going to go on for the rest of our lives – there's nothing we can do about it.

I am going to call my puppy Scarlet, after Scarlet O'Hara in *Gone with the Wind*.

1940

I walk across the cliffs to visit the spaniel puppies today. They are with their mother asleep in a big cardboard box in the kitchen, four of them all muddled up together so you can't tell one from the other. There were only two bitches apparently and one of those died. So I am to have one of the boy ones. Black and white with long silky ears. Very sweet.

Bellman – I love him already.

It's still winter – well, spring – and we are teaching my puppy to swim, in a little stream almost on the beach near the golf course. Ma says he'll get pneumonia because it's so cold, but I think he enjoys it. His name comes from the Bellman in Edward Lear's poem *The Hunting of the Snark*, my favourite poem. I took him to school in my satchel yesterday, and Miss Tearle sent me home. School is so boring. I don't know what they are talking about half the time. Miss Tearle can't keep order.

Ma got furious with me today, but it wasn't my fault. First she lost the ration books – she thinks she's left them in a shopping bag up at the garage. Then the kettle boiled dry and from now on we are going to have to use a saucepan because nobody has kettles for sale any more. Then Julyan climbed on to the work top to get at the scissors (forbidden) and upset the tin of golden syrup (didn't notice), and it just slowly dripped through everything into the knife drawer so that all the knives and the tea towels underneath were stuck together. After that he ran out into the road and wouldn't come back, and Ma couldn't catch him (very, very annoying). Simon and I were over in Roland's garden, and by the time we came home Ma had finally caught him and stuck him in his little bedroom with the door shut. There's a step down into his room from the passage outside, and he is not tall enough yet to reach up to the door latch, so if the door is shut he can't get out. He was still screaming blue murder when I put my head in at the window. He looked a bit pathetic, red face covered in tears, so I felt sorry for him (he's still quite small after all, and he is my little brother).

'Julyan,' I said, 'look…if you pull the chair over and stand on it, you can reach the latch.' The screaming stopped at once and of course he was out of his room in a flash. But Ma was walking along behind me and heard what I said. Was she angry, Christopher Columbus! She came after me hitting me round the ears and shouting at the top of her voice – I had to run away from her into the garden like Julyan. I explained, from a distance, that I didn't know about the golden syrup and everything else, and then I got on my bike and cycled up to the garage to see if Grace Hawkey had found the ration books (she had). By the time I got back, Ma had calmed down. Simon said we would have to fix a chain and padlock on the outside of Julyan's door, and that made her laugh. This evening she's OK. (Actually, when I think about it, all she has to do is take his chair away.)

A massive balk of timber about ten feet long has washed up in Fox Cove, and has been sloshing around there for a week or so. Jeremy and Kenneth, Roland, and me are going to try and haul it round to Treyarnon and sell it to Mr Chandler who farms there. At high tide two days ago we skipped school, swam out to the further side of the cove and pushed it back to where we could get it up on the rocks above high water (you have to leave 'found' driftwood above the high-water mark, because then everyone knows that someone has put it there and is coming back for it). Jeremy's father says that if we want we can borrow the dinghy he keeps in the hotel garage, and row round to Foxy.

On Saturday, we take the dinghy out on a flood tide, and then row round the headland. The tide is already very high near the rocks and there is no anchor and nothing to moor the dinghy to, so Roland stays in the boat. The wood is tremendously heavy, but with Jeremy at one end and me and Kenneth at the other we start pushing and rolling it down to the water. It makes a terrific splash and disappears for a moment, then bobs up again wallowing and turning as if it were alive. We are standing around trying to decide how to attach the line, when there is some shouting. Two men are coming down the cliff path high above us, and even from here we can all see that they look pretty rough.

'They are after the wood!' Jeremy says.

'It's ours – they can't have it! Come on!' Kenneth gets into the boat with Roland, and grabs the towing line. The rest of us jump into the water (cold), and try to manoeuvre the timber so we can fix the line to it. But it is rolling a lot and so big we can't get the line round it. The two men are running down the narrow path yelling and waving their arms. They will be here in a minute or two, so we start pushing it out through the water while Kenneth rows ahead, and soon we are swimming in deep green water shoving the wood ahead in front. Unless the pair on the rocks are going to jump in and swim after us, there is nothing they can do. One of them is still shouting.

'Stop there! You kids, just stop there!'

'Not bloody likely!' Jeremy says.

We get the line tied on finally, and then start to row. Even with two of us rowing, it takes quite a time. Once, the line comes loose, and Roland and I have to dive in and swim round and round in circles getting it fixed on again. We get back to the beach as the tide is ebbing, and I have a nasty feeling that the men will be waiting for us there, but all we see is Jeremy's father walking his spaniels. Mr Chandler is very pleased and gives us five pounds! He is going to cut up the timber for gate posts. He says he'll give us a good price again if ever we find any more timber he can use on the farm.

Mr Prynne is in the warren opposite the bungalow with his dog and his traps today. He's got a big pile of rabbits, and he shows us how to catch them by making a wire snare to hide in the grass at the entrance to a burrow. We watch him for a bit but everything is quiet, and we don't catch anything. He says come back later and it'll be swarming with 'em. But we go swimming instead.

Roland and Kenneth can't stop laughing and giggling and mucking about at the moment. They make up silly names and phrases, and then say them again and again and again until one or both are rolling about in hysterics. 'Boil me dry, you crumpled Craddock,' is the new one – or 'feak and weeble' instead of weak and feeble. What's so funny about that? The made up words in *The Hunting of the Snark* are much better.

Ma doesn't have much over for pocket money, so Simon has thought of a good way to get hold of a bit more money.

Most of the groundsmen have been called up and there are only a few golfers around at the moment, so we often take short cuts across the golf course on the way to the headland. Because it's such a large course, most of the greens are out of sight of the teeing-off squares; so the club has kindly stuck white-painted metal arrows flat into the ground pointing which way to drive the ball. Simon has had the clever idea of switching all the arrows to point in the wrong direction – carefully planned so that the ball will end up in the brambles or the long grass. The golfers don't know the course like we do, and after they have given up looking and gone on, we find the balls quite easily (we know where to look). Then we offer them for sale to the next lot, at sixpence each! Good for us and the golfers, as golf balls are in short supply and cost two shillings. (We don't tell Ma about this scheme.)

At teatime today, Ma informs me that after the end of this term Miss Tearle doesn't want me at her school any more, because I lead the little ones on and, she says, use bad language. (I don't remember doing that. What language?) So I have to go to another school over in Rock, starting at the beginning of the summer term. Boarding.

I am not at all pleased by this news.

This afternoon the Dragon caught me in her garden. On the way back from school, Kenneth, Simon, the O'Brien boys, Roland and me stopped to play on the bit of waste land between the golf course and her back garden, and Roland kicked the ball over her hedge by mistake. The others say they are too frightened to go into her garden, but I climb through a little gap in the hedge, and am poking about looking for the ball when, suddenly, there she is, shouting at me.

'I am sorry, but we have lost our ball Mrs H,' I say – I can hear the others giggling on the other side of the hedge. 'Please could–'

'Rude child! How dare you come in here without asking–'

'Rude yourself,' I say grabbing the ball and running away from her and through the gate. We can hear her shouting and yelling from halfway up the lane, old misery!

Ma says I have to write a letter of apology. (I'll write it, but somehow it will disappear on the way.)

I am to go to a girls' school which has been evacuated to Rock called Dormy House. I have to wear a uniform. Ma has found a second-hand one because she hasn't the money to buy it new, and I must tie my hair back and look tidy. She has lost the ration books again.

Simon has got hold of a big ex-RAF lamp. It is a bit dented on one side, but shines an incredibly bright white beam of light, so we are going lamping tonight. Much easier than fiddling around with bits of wire.

As soon as it is dark, Simon takes his rifle. (Maybe it's an air gun? Where did he get it from anyway? He didn't buy it.) I carry the lamp, and we walk down to the long rough bit of ground between 'Sea Spell' and the dunes. We don't talk and we haven't got shoes on, so we don't make much noise. After about ten minutes Simon whispers 'switch on!' and there, dotted all over the grass, are the rabbits. I shine the light in their faces – rabbits can't move if they get caught in a strong light – and Simon starts shooting. We get ten. Quite good.

We give Ma two and hang up the others in the garage. Instead of going to school the next day, we bike into Padstow with the rabbits over our handlebars. Mr Keast the butcher is very pleased, gives us one and nine pence a rabbit! Take off three pence for the cartridge, and that's seventeen shillings and five pence. Not bad!

Ma is listening to the wireless in the sitting room when we get home, and I can tell from her face that she's worried. Everything's fine she says when I ask. But I know that's not true. It's the war, I expect, but she looks so miserable I give her my rabbit money as a present. Talking of rabbits, Billy (our cat) keeps bringing in baby rabbits. He eats the head and the front legs, but leaves the rest. Often, if I look under the bed before getting into it at night, there will be half a rabbit and perhaps a pair of ears there. Unfortunately, I don't think Mr Keast would be interested in chewed-up half rabbits…

Pouring rain, a gale blowing and it's the beginning of the summer term at the 'Dormy House School for Girls'. The farmer Frank Andrew has taken my trunk over there because farmers have petrol coupons and he had to take some bullocks to St Minver, but Ma and I are walking up to the post office to get the bus into Padstow, where the ferry will take us over to Rock. Then there is a twenty-minute walk up the road to the school. We'll be soaked by the time we get there.

Big Bill Lindsey, in his long white waders and yellow oilskins, is at the wheel today, with a crowd of Wrens on board. It is high tide and the wind is whipping up the water into waves which keep blowing up into sheets of spray and drenching everyone. Each time it happens, all the Wrens scream. Considering they are in the navy they don't seem very used to being at sea. When we get to the other side, I jump down into the water and pull the landing plank forward, while Bill keeps the ferry pointing up into the wind.

'I'll give your little maid a job any time Mrs Watts,' Bill says, laughing. But Ma is in a bad mood.

'Just *look* at her shoes! *New*! Well, wet or dry she is going to school, Bill. Knock some sense into her.' Bill looks at me and gives me a wink.

I am home for half-term from horrible Barmy House, and Ma is still worried. The British army is stuck on a beach called Dunkirk on the other side of the channel – Germans on one side, sea on the other. But when the fish man comes round ringing his bell, he tells us that all the small boats, including the lifeboats, right round the east coast are getting ready to fetch them home.

'They'll be bringing 'em back, you see my lover,' he says to Ma, and drives off ringing his bell out of the window of his van and shouting: 'F-i-i-ishh-O! F-i-i-ishh-O!' You can hear him for miles.

Even at half-term, we have to water the vegetables Ma is growing. Every evening! It takes ages, bucket after bucket. When we have done enough, Ma reads to us. It's *Dombey and Son* at the moment. This evening I am watering the carrots, and Freathy Tippet walks past with his roadman's shovel on his shoulder and tells me that all the east coast lifeboats, plus the Royal Navy and hundreds of little boats as far away as Whitby, have ferried the Dunkirk soldiers home. So the fish man was right!

Barmy House is like my first boarding school, but not so big. I am not frightened all the time like I used to be at my other school, and we don't have to wear stockings in summer. It is so boring I think I am going to die.

This afternoon, for games, we went swimming in Daimer Bay. To get to the beach by road takes about half an hour. Running across the field at the back of the school and down through the marram grass and dunes is about ten minutes. Of course we go by road, walking two by two in the hot sun carrying our swimming costumes and towels. When we get to the beach, we are told to undress 'in the shelter of the dunes, modestly, girls'. Then we are given a lecture about 'keeping within our depth' – not very difficult, as the spit of sand that stretches out from Daimer Bay towards the opposite side of the estuary makes it shallow anyway. I lie down in the water and start swimming (knocking my knees on the sandy bottom it is so shallow), and then swim on a bit more, and a bit more as it gets gradually deeper. It is so cool and lovely in the water with nobody else near me that very soon I am almost halfway to the Padstow side. Back on the beach, the people have all become dots, including Miss Baxter, the games mistress. So I start swimming back. What a palaver! Miss Baxter has waded out (can she swim, I wonder?) and is shrieking at me: 'putting my life in danger', 'disobedience', 'bad example' – everything you can think of. And I will 'certainly be severely punished' when she reports me, screech, screech.

After tea, the housemistress lectures me for at least half an hour, and then I have to sit and write out 'I must listen to members of staff when they are speaking to me', and 'I must obey school rules whatever I think of them' two hundred times. I draw a very small picture of Bellman at the bottom, looking up at all the lines and making a funny face. When Miss Baxter sees that she makes me do it all again without Bellman.

Ten o'clock and I am stuck in class B's room with the vicar – he comes in on Tuesday mornings to teach us about the Bible, droning on and on although no one is listening. (If you created the vicar for propaganda purposes, God, you didn't do a very good job.) Through the open window I can see blue water between the sandhills shimmering in the hot sun. At break I have to stay behind and copy out a map of the Holy Land, as the first one I did was 'untidy' – one small blot in the corner which I turned into a picture of Bellman looking saintly, smiling, with a halo. The vicar is having coffee in the staff common room, and without thinking much about it I climb out of the window – which is at the back of the school, so nobody sees me – and then run as fast as I can across the field and down the hill on the hot sand of the dunes and the beach. I am lucky; Bill Lindsey and the ferry are approaching.

'You off home then?' he says, laughing.

'I've forgotten my fare money.'

'Pay next time?' and he winks at me again.

It takes a long time to walk across the cliffs to the bungalow, and when I get there everyone except Bellman is out. He is *so* pleased to see me, and I am very pleased to see him. He's grown! I make myself a big plate of bread and jam, and lie on the sofa with Bellman licking my face, looking at the ceiling. The knots in the wood turn into eyes or faces, or animals writhing about like snakes, if you stare long enough at them. The phone, which is a payphone in one of the bedrooms, rings.

'Mrs Watts?'

'She is out. Can I take a message?'

'Will you ask her to telephone the Dormy House School as soon as she returns, please?'

'I've just remembered, Mrs Watts is away…for a long time… er…'

Suddenly, Ma comes into the room with Julyan. Unlike Bellman, she is not pleased to see me at all, and says that in an hour's time the last bus goes into Padstow, and that I must go back on it and then take the ferry.

'But I hate it there!'

'You *have* to go to school!'

'Why?'

Ma sits down on the sofa with a bump.

'Paris has fallen,' she says.

Matron looks as if she'd like to kill me, but otherwise nothing much happens when I reappear at Barmy House. After two days, I am told that the headmistress wants to see me in her room, go and wait outside.

Miss Griesbach, the headmistress, is a small plump lady with white hair done up in a bun on the top of her head, long flowing clothes, and a black velvet ribbon round her neck. I recognise which one she is but I have never spoken to her before, or she to me.

'Sit down please,' she says. 'I don't think we have met. Would you like a biscuit?'

It's a nice room with books and flowers on her table, French windows out on to grass and a view of sand dunes and the sea. I sit munching my biscuit wondering what she will say next.

'I am sorry you are not happy here, Marjorie-Ann. Is that why you ran away?'

'I am bored,' I say, thinking she'll really boil over at that. But she sits looking at me and saying nothing for a minute or two, and then she says 'I am not really surprised. I don't think this is the right school for you.'

My heart gives a lurch. Ma is going to be absolutely frothing furious. First the Evacuee School and now this!

'I have had a talk with your mother and she agrees with me. She is going to take you to see a school I have suggested where I think you would be much happier. It's expensive but there is an art scholarship. You are good at drawing, so perhaps you should have a go? Meantime I think you should be a weekly boarder – on condition you work hard for the scholarship and don't run away again.' She holds out her hand. 'Is that a bargain?' We shake hands (nothing else I can do really). 'Being bored is being lazy,' she says. 'You won't be bored if you work hard.' Actually, Miss Griesbach is quite nice.

It is such a hot day we bike over to one of the coves to climb down the cliffs and swim. At low tide, the Minnies is nothing but boulders and rocks scattered about over a big rambling broken up basin. But when the sea comes in, all that is covered, 'drowned', except for the highest parts which become islands and ledges, and from where one can dive deep into dark green transparent water.

Roland and Simon are investigating a steep stack of rock on the far side of the cove, but I climb down into the water slowly and carefully. It is very quiet. I am just lying there looking up at the sun and paddling gently, when a head pops up about thirty yards away. A grey seal, looking at me. I call very softly to him – Freathy Tippet told me that seals are curious and will sometimes come quite near if you whistle or call to them. This one disappears, and I think he has gone. Then he surfaces again in a different place, but nearer, head well up and still gazing at me intently. I go on calling and he goes on diving and then reappearing a little closer and a little closer, until, gradually he is only a few yards away, so near that I can see his whiskers, soft brown eyes, grey freckles near his nose. We look at each other for a minute or two, and then with a little splash he's gone. Lucky that I left Bellman at home, as he would have gone mad, barking and chasing, wanting to play. I often take Bellman swimming, as he loves the water. But I have to swim very fast, as he paddles along after me and I get scratches down my back from his claws.

Yesterday, I had just finished giving Julyan a swimming lesson in one of the rock pools at Treyarnon and we were on the beach getting dressed, when we heard the noise of approaching aircraft. Recently there have been a lot of scares about German pilots coming in suddenly over the beaches to strafe and machine gun the civilians on them, so all the mothers jumped to their feet in a panic, calling to their children. But it was only three Spitfires, flying in very fast and low over the sea and then, as soon as they got to the beach, swooping up above our heads with a terrific roar and flashing silver in the sun as the pilots turned their machines over and over in a victory roll. Very exciting, and all the children, including me and Julyan, cheered. But one of the mothers said that she'd had enough without these 'high jinks' frightening everyone, and she was going to complain up at the camp.

Simon keeps saying he is going into the air force as soon as he possibly can, and Julyan says he will too. (He is five!)

It's holiday time and we are off on our bicycles a lot – very few cars, no petrol or coupons. Today, as a treat, we are all going to bicycle over to Zennor, to visit a friend of Ma's, Mrs Sloman. She is a farmer's wife and runs the Tinner's Arms and the post office at Zennor. Julyan is too little, so he is staying with Uncle Christopher, Ma's other brother: his house in London has been bombed, so they are living in their bungalow here for a few weeks. But Simon and me and the eldest Selby-Smith boy George are all bicycling to Zennor with Ma.

Zennor is an extremely long way, a lot of slow, uphill roads on the other side of St Ives. George and I go on ahead, but Simon and Ma lag behind, as Simon is tired and his legs hurt. Mrs Sloman, who knew my grandmother when she stayed here to write one of her books, has a huge high tea waiting for us when we arrive: ham, eggs, toasted cheese, home-grown radishes and cucumber, saffron bread, cream, strawberry jam, and tinned peaches and custard. All off the ration because it's a farm.

Simon isn't hungry, though, and looks pale and miserable, and next day he doesn't feel well and has a temperature. On Monday Ma gets the doctor to come out from St Ives and it turns out he's got German measles! Mrs Sloman says that she doesn't know whether 'their Kevin', who is quite old and a bit funny in the head and works on the farm, or Mr Sloman, have ever had German or any other kind of measles. And she doesn't want them getting anything now, as who else would do the work on the farm? So Simon and Ma have to move into a B&B next door, and George and I bike back home on our own!

Some soldiers come today and begin to build a concrete pillbox the other side of our garden hedge overlooking the road coming up from the sea. First they dig out a sort of pit in amongst the thorn that grows on the small triangle of ground there. Then, this concrete cabin with slits for windows gets built. Ma is very upset, red in the face and tears. But the sergeant says, 'Don't worry madam, we are going to mine the sandhills, and put barbed wire along the beach. They'll never get through all that!' (He means the Germans.)

He says Bellman is the best-looking springer he has ever seen.

Ma looks worried *all* the time nowadays. I feel quite sorry for her. It's because the Germans might invade Cornwall up our road. Kenneth, who lives very near the beach, says his father is trying to get him and his mum and the other children out to Canada on a ship. They go in convoys, with British destroyers protecting them from the U-boats. His father is in the navy, so I suppose it's easy for them.

Something called the Blitz is going on in London. (It started in July.) German planes coming over every night and bombing everyone. I am glad we are not still at Holly Place – it has probably been bombed flat by now.

There is barbed wire, double rolls and rolls of it stretching across from side to side on the beach. The sandhills behind are full of mines and, blocking the path down, the soldiers have left big triangular blocks of cement called 'Devil's Teeth' to stop the German tanks. You can still get through by walking along a narrow cleft where a stream trickles down from the golf course, but it's a long way round. The soldiers have built a pillbox among the grass and bramble there too, and sometimes we light fires in it and fry limpets and mussels. They are too disgusting for us to eat, but Bellman gobbles them up.

After we are in bed today, Ma has a visitor. The wife of Wing Commander Somebody. She has a voice like a foghorn and Ma is shouting because she's nervous, but you can hear everything through the wooden walls of the bungalow anyway.

Ma: 'Yes, I am thinking of taking the children away from the danger of invasion to my cousins' in North Wales. It's a big old rectory…'

Mrs WCS: 'My dear, is that wise? These are just rumours flying about.'

'But you've seen all the sea defences? Barbed wire, tank traps? The dunes are mined. Obviously they are expecting an invasion here.'

'Defences are being put up everywhere, as a precaution. I do beg you not to give in to hysteria. People like us have to set an example.'

'You can set an example if you like, but I want my children in a safe place.'

At this point, they go into the kitchen, and I can't hear so well. When they come back, the conversation is about whether it would be a good idea to go to Canada or even America, in a convoy like Kenneth's mother. Mrs Wing Commander doesn't seem so much against that. Perhaps she is planning to go in a convoy herself? Anyway, I fell asleep.

The next day, Simon and I decide that we don't want to go anywhere, and if Ma really goes ahead with her idea of leaving Cornwall – either for Wales or in a convoy to Canada – we will go and hide in one of the caves above Fox or Pepper Cove, just until she has missed the departure time. Then we will come back. We are going to collect some tins of food and store them in one of the caves, just in case.

'I'll take my knife with the corkscrew and the tin opener,' Simon says. 'And we'll need our bikes. We'll have to get our water from the stream.'

But in the end, we don't need any of it. The cousins in North Wales have got too many evacuees staying already, and one of the ships carrying families going to Canada has been torpedoed and blown up – everyone drowned. So Ma has thought better of that plan, although she is still worried.

There is an air battle going on between German bombers and the RAF somewhere over England at this very moment, Kent I think. I hope our side wins. Roland's elder brother is flying a Spitfire, and cousin Pearl's twins – who have only just left school – have been called up!

Ma has got a job. She is a billeting officer for evacuee children sent down to Cornwall to get away from the bombing, the Blitz, so she gets coupons for her car. On Friday evening we go up to the village hall to see some of them arrive.

The WVS ladies are bustling about and it is gloomy and dark because of the rain; the evacuee children are standing crowded together like sheep, lit by the light from the hall. They look small and tired and some of the little ones are crying. I can see the tickets pinned on them saying who they are. One little girl has lost her ticket and can't remember her name. Albert Sandry, who built the wall down to the sea on the other side of our road, and Mrs Albert are there, and the Pitmans, the Bennetts, Mr Old from the shop, even Mr Curragh who lives in two railway carriages with Mrs C and all their children up beyond the post office. We don't have room for anyone extra, but some of the big houses near the beach could take in a family or two.

Mr Sandry is leaving with two red-haired girls, the bigger one carrying her sister. 'We wanted a boy,' he says to Ma. 'But these 'ere won't be separated. So we're takin' 'em both.'

Captain Farquhar is standing there looking important in his uniform. He works up at the Fleet Air Arm, and has a huge house down on one of the bays. He tells Ma, 'I only want *gentleman boys* Mrs Watts, is that understood?' But I don't think she hears him, there is such a noise – the WVS ladies shouting out names, children crying.

At the weekend, Captain Farquhar calls. The two evacuee boys he's been allocated have chopped up all the deckchairs stacked in his garage waiting to be repaired and burned them for fun. Now they've run away back to London.

'I'm making a complaint, Mrs Watts. You will have to report it.'

'Gerald and his brother are your responsibility while they are your guests, Captain Farquhar,' Ma says. 'You must inform the police–'

'I haven't got time to chase young criminals round the countryside, Mrs Watts. There is a war on in case you hadn't heard!' And with that he marches out.

'He'll get a whole family next time,' mutters Ma.

Violet, Mrs Gammon's cleaner, comes to see Ma today. The Gammons have got a spare house for their chauffeur at the end of their drive, called 'the Rashers' (Mrs Gammon's idea of a joke) – empty because of the war. Well, it *was* empty. Now it's got two evacuee families in it, the O'Reillys. Two mothers and seven children and a baby just born. The children are filthy and 'do things' in their beds, Violet says.

'And Mrs Watts, all of them have got nits in their hair, and are passing them on up at the school! Mrs Gammon's doing war work in London and I don't know what to do!'

'A nit comb, methylated spirits, and make sure they all get their heads washed – several times,' Ma says. 'The mothers too, Violet.' As she is leaving, Ma asks how Captain Farquhar is getting on with his new evacuees. (Violet cleans his big house down on the bay as well as the two Gammon houses.)

'He's got the nine O'Reilly cousins now,' Violet says. '*And* their old grandma. It's a judgement Mrs Watts.' (Violet is a Jehovah's Witness.)

The rolls of barbed wire and tank traps make it awkward getting down to the beach. You can squeeze through, but the wire tears your clothes and then Ma gets furious. So usually we walk down Blind Lane, across the sand dunes at the bottom and then along the bed of the stream trickling down from the golf course. Quite a rigmarole. Today Kenneth changed that.

Mrs Hainselin's terrier Jobo often goes off by himself, rabbiting in the warren or on the golf course. Today, he attaches himself to us while we are on our way to the beach, and starts ferreting about in the marram grass near the wire. Roland picks up a stick and throws it for him to 'fetch'. Jobo loves that.

'Watch this!' Kenneth says, and throws the stick to the other side of the fence and the barbed wire. The fence looks strong, but the sand has fallen away into a sort of gully at one place, and Jobo soon gets through. We hold our breath, expecting an explosion, one of the mines going off as Jobo whizzes through the wire to get the stick, but nothing happens. He goes backward and forwards in all directions as each of us has a go, and after a while there is a broad track of dog footmarks in and out of the wire on both sides.

'No mines there!' Kenneth says. 'We'll get some pliers and clip a path through!'

In the evening there are two explosions – and of course, immediately I think someone has gone down there and been blown up! But actually it is a German bomber on the way home from Plymouth off-loading his two remaining bombs on the lighthouse. (He missed.)

Billy brings in half a baby rabbit again. He only eats the front half, and the back bit – legs, innards, poor little white scut – he leaves under my bed as a present. Why does he always choose my bed?

Two parcels from Egypt today – Uncle Toby! One of them had a grey and blue Shetland rug and six pairs of silk stockings in it, the other food: some Argentine beef in two square tins, tins of butter, some tea, a box of Elva plums and about twenty thick bars of chocolate. Ma is very pleased but worried about how to keep the butter and chocolate fresh as we don't have a fridge, just the meat safe. In the end Mr Ford, who sometimes does six hundred strokes on the pump to get water up from the well for us, comes to dig a deep pit, sandy but quite cool. It's going to be a sort of underground cupboard where we can store things – the tins of meat, for example. I don't know about the chocolate; she wouldn't tell us where she was going to keep that. (Ma loves chocolate, and sometimes eats our sweet ration if we are not looking!) 'I think I'll manage,' she says, laughing. 'Somehow or other!'

I am boiling the saucepan for tea, when the electricity goes off. Mr Ford says it is just a fuse, and he'll mend it. But nobody can find the pliers. So I know that Roland or

Simon or one of the others has been down clipping a path through the wire.

Roland's elder brother – the one in the RAF who flies Spitfires – has been killed. Ma says he is a hero, and keeps shaking her head and crying all day. I feel sad too.

Ma and I make a 'stocking' for Julyan – actually a large army sock stuffed full of bits and pieces she has been keeping for him: some colouring crayons, a magnet, a bell for the trike he is going to get, even a tangerine she got from somewhere. He woke up at half past four to see if Father Christmas had been, and stayed awake until it was getting light. Ma gave him a tricycle (second-hand from one of Mr Curragh's hundreds of children), and I got a leather collar with Bellman's name on it, a fountain pen (very good for drawing), and a pink woolly jersey that Uncle Toby had sent in the Egyptian parcel without me noticing. Simon got a torch with several batteries, a set of screwdrivers, and an Airfix model of a Hurricane to make. We gave Ma some scented bath essence and a piece of lavender soap that Roland's aunt had given him and he didn't want, and took her breakfast in bed. Now, at midday the sun is shining and we are going to have a Christmas picnic on the beach!

We trek over to Treyarnon and collect as much driftwood as we can get together to light a really enormous fire, and then Simon and me – and Bellman – rush into the water. Ma says it's too cold for her, and stays on the edge with Julyan, as he only paddles. (Compared to the cold air, the water feels warm!) While we are swimming it starts to snow, but by that time the fire is huge and so fierce and hot that it dries us very quickly. Then we have a hot picnic: soup, sausages and bread with bits of toasted cheese fried at the side of the fire, slices of Christmas pudding heated in their tins, and pieces of Uncle Toby's chocolate with Elva plums. Julyan drops his Christmas pudding in the sand, but I wash it in the sea for him and it is OK – anyway, he eats it.

By the time we've finished everything and had a climb up Trethias Island it is beginning to get dark. So we pack up and walk home across the black cliffs, looking back at the pinpoint of fire glowing on the beach and singing 'Hark the Herald Angels Sing' at the top of our voices.

1941

Mrs Hainselin's terrier, Jobo, has disappeared. He was rabbiting somewhere on the sandhills near the barbed wire, and one of the rabbit burrows must have collapsed in on him. They could hear him barking, but nobody would go to dig him out because of the mines. If it had been Bellman I would have gone.

We got shot at today. Simon and I had left our bikes in the hedge near Trevose Farm, and were on the headland walking towards the lighthouse when a Dornier droned over us quite low. We were just standing gaping up at the swastikas, when there was a rattling tat-tat-tat noise, and the turf in front of us jumped up in a semicircle. I couldn't think what it was, until Simon shouted: 'They're shooting at us! Get down! Quick!' and dived sideways into some long grass between the gorse. I jumped in after him and we watched the plane fly on out across the sea. What a relief! Gorse is like bunches of needles, and there's nowhere else to hide out here if the Dornier had come back for another go.

When we get home, Ma tells us what Grace Hawkey has just told her: that some German planes flew over Newquay at twelve o'clock today and machine gunned the main street just when the children were coming out of school. A lot of them were killed, so I suppose we had a lucky escape.

Violet's brother Horace has been reported missing. He is – I mean was – in the Merchant Navy.

That's two of her brothers.

One of my drawings gets first prize in the mid-term exhibition at Barmy House – only because the other drawings are so bad! So I have put it in my scholarship folder with about twenty others, and today we are travelling up to the school for me to take the entrance examination and show them my drawings and everything. We are staying with friends of Ma's who have a bookshop in the town nearby. I wish it was over. Supposing they don't like me? It all takes a long time and is quite embarrassing. I have to do some tests and the examination, talk to the art master and then, in a few weeks, they will decide, and the bursar will write to Ma to say whether my drawings are good enough. If I don't get the scholarship, I can't go to the school which is a pity, because the swimming pool and high diving boards are the best I've ever seen. Out of doors and really big.

I spend most of the morning doing these weird tests and answering questions. Then it's time to go to the head of art, a grumpy old man in the studio, a hut on its own down near the swimming pool.

'Well, come in, come in…' I put my folder of drawings on the table in front of him. 'What's your name? What? Speak up? I can't hear you!' When I tell him my name loudly and clearly, he says, 'Watts? Hmm…any relation of Arthur Watts?'

'My father,' I say. He turns round and really looks at me, seems quite pleased. Apparently they were friends at some art school together – the Slade.

'Arthur Watts was *your* father?'

'Yes.'

'Can you draw as well as him?'

'No,' I say, because of course I can't draw as well as that. He looks at my drawings, asks a lot of different questions, and after a few minutes more I go back to Ma feeling very disappointed. Because if I have to draw as well as my father, I won't get the scholarship. She says we will have to wait and see, but now her friends are going to take us to *Gone with the Wind* as a treat! So then I cheer up. (It will be the third time I've seen it.) Clark Gable is my most favourite man in all the world.

Ma says the Germans have invaded Russia. When we get home, I look it up on Simon's world atlas. It is absolutely huge – halfway round the world. Keep going and they'll get to China.

Another raid. Roland and I have biked over to Newquay, and we can see the German plane lumbering round and round dropping its bombs, but this time some fighters come streaking out of the sky from above the clouds. The bomber turns to head off towards the sea, but too slowly. There is the sound of gunfire, and suddenly it begins to dip down towards the flat blue, black smoke pouring out behind. It hits the sea with a terrific thump and a column of water shoots up into the sky.

'Good,' Roland says.

'What's happened to the pilot?'

'Dead,' he says.

'Good,' I say – but actually, it doesn't feel 'good' that somebody who was alive a minute ago is now dead, even if he is a German. Although on the headland the other day they were trying to kill us! And they have killed Roland's brother. So it serves them right. (What is it like to be burned and drowned at the same time?)

A letter has come to say that I have been given an art scholarship! I *can* go to the new school, and I am to start in the autumn! So, at the end of the summer term, I am leaving Barmy House and we are going to move to Hertfordshire. Ma has got friends there and another job, and it is nearer to the new school.

I start smiling a lot because I am thinking about the huge outdoors swimming pool with its diving boards and green water.

Last night, we saw a policeman with a van, and Ralph Pitman and Mr Rabey in their fishing gear – long waders and waterproofs – over by the hotel garages. I asked them if they had been fishing, and what they had caught. But they didn't really answer, just said to go back into the house and stay there. Today, Ma told us that a German airman had been washed up on the beach, and had been put in one of the garages for the night before they took him away to be buried. She thinks he is from the bomber we saw shot down.

Ma and Una – Mrs Hawke's eldest daughter, who is coming with us as a mother's help – are packing the car, and Julyan is helping (which means not helping and sending everybody crazy). He is very excited because Ma is driving him and Una up to Hertfordshire to the new house. As it is such a small car and we have so much stuff as well as three people and a dog and a cat, there isn't room for me and Simon. So we are going to take our bicycles on the train through Plymouth to Totnes; stay with Ma's friend Mrs Davies, the admiral's wife, and then cycle on the next day to the Bliss's near Bruton. They won't be there (Mrs B and the children are in America), but we can stay in their house. After that, we go on by train to Winchester, then I think it is Reading and Hertford, and cycle from there to 'Van Tort's Cottage' in Sawbridgeworth, which is where we are going to live. Ma is worried about us going to Plymouth because of the bombing there. But that's mostly at night, so we'll just stay on the train until it gets to Totnes. Ma will drive up all the way to Hertfordshire and be at Van Tort's Cottage when we arrive in four days' time.

At Padstow, our cycles go in the luggage van, and Ma tips the guard to keep an eye on us and make sure we get out at Totnes. She needn't have bothered, as he leaves the train at Plymouth, having forgotten all about us.

Plymouth water is crammed with ships and anti-aircraft balloons flying above them. Some of the docks and cranes, and the houses on either side of the railway line, are smashed to bits. Just rubble and stone, bricks, broken slates and timbers all piled up together where the houses used to be. (I am glad Ma's bungalow is not in Plymouth!)

Admiral Davies lives in Dittisham, and we have to cycle there from Totnes. It is a long way – about fifteen miles – and hilly. We have to cross the river Dart with the bikes by ferry, and then find the house on the other side.

Macadam roads are burning hot in summer. The tar of this one is melting and the backs of my hands are sunburned and sore. I try and hold the handlebars from underneath, but it is difficult. We are almost the only people on the road (hardly a car anywhere), so sometimes we cross over to the wrong side where it is shady to keep in the cool. At one village we ask a lady which way for Dittisham, and she gives us directions and some lovely cool lemonade. Homemade, she said.

At last, we are whizzing through a cool tunnel of trees overhanging a steep hill dropping down and down to a little grassy jetty. A notice with a bell on the end of a rope next to it says: 'FERRY. Ring the bell.' We do this several times, but nothing happens. So we sit on the grass and wait – what else can we do? We can't swim across because of the bicycles, and we can't go back. Simon rings the bell again. Then I ring it. After we have waited for at least three quarters of an hour, the ferry man appears on the opposite side of the river, rowing a grey dory.

'You'm in a terrible hurry,' he says when he reaches us.

Admiral Davies comes home from work in a dark blue naval truck with a driver and a red ensign on the bonnet. He is going to a meeting in Bristol early tomorrow, so he will give us a lift and put us on the right road for Bruton – where we are staying the night. We have spam shepherd's pie for supper, my favourite.

In the morning, the driver loads our bicycles into the back of the truck and we drive off. Mrs Davies says that Bill, her husband, would like to take us all the way, but he can't because of the meeting. She puts calamine lotion on my hands and bandages them to keep the sun off, and makes us some sandwiches.

Bruton is further than Dittisham, and as the signposts are being painted out or removed because the Germans might invade it is more difficult to find our way. At one place we ask a man on a steamroller which way to go, and he says he is going to Bruton himself and will give us a lift. But as he is only going three quarters of a mile each hour, we say no thanks. At another place – the bottom of a road climbing up a long steep hill – we grab hold at the back of a hay cart behind a farm tractor, and get pulled right up to the top! In the valley below us, faintly, we can still hear the steamroller grinding along.

The Bliss house is on its own in the middle of fields and woods, all glass and straight lines, white, modern, at the end of a long drive. There is nobody there, but the housekeeper has left us a note and there is bread and butter, fruit and cold chicken in the fridge. We sit on the fur rug in the big drawing room eating chicken with our fingers, and watching the moths attracted by the light fluttering and crawling up the other side of the enormous plate glass windows. Behind them, the country is black and quiet.

It's lucky Ma has so many friends and relations all over the country. After Bruton it is Mrs Pidcock in Winchester, and the next day, when we have eaten a giant breakfast, she puts us on the train to Hertford. In order to avoid London (because of air raids), we are going to have to change trains twice, and as the carriages are full up with soldiers going to Aldershot, Mrs P asks the guard if we and our bicycles can travel with him in the guard's van. He has a dog travelling with him and four crates of homing pigeons as well as

84

ordinary luggage, but he says there's room for us too and that he will see us on to the Hertford train. Once we get to Hertford town, we have to cycle on to Sawbridgeworth – where Ma will be waiting at Van Tort's Cottage.

Mrs P buys us some doughnuts and some slab cake at the station café, the guard blows his whistle and off we go.

Seven hours later, and we have transferred to the Hertford train. It is stifling hot and I could drink a bath full of water. Something has happened further up the line and we have been sitting here for hours. 'Jerry,' the guard says. 'Air raid, can't you hear it?' And there is a sort of thumping bumping yak-yak noise in the distance. In the end we don't puff into Hertford station until about nine o'clock.

It is cooler at last, a lovely soft calm evening thick with moths, the lanes sweet smelling as we pedal along. The thumping noise and the ack-ack guns are much louder out here, and as it gets dark we can see searchlight beams crisscrossing the sky over to the right. London? It must be.

At last we cycle into Sawbridgeworth, although it is so late by now it's not easy to see anything much. Finding Van Tort's Cottage isn't easy either, but in the end we get there – a black and white half timbered building in a row of cottages, all looking rather dark and uninhabited. We bang on the door, and bang again, but nobody comes. Just when we are thinking we've got the wrong place, the wrong village even, a woman appears from next door.

'The lady's been delayed,' she says. 'Are you the children?'

We say yes we are, and she says 'I have got some milk for you' and gives us a jug of milk and some keys. Then she shuts her door.

Of course we have never been in the cottage before, so we switch the lights on to look around. Immediately there are shouts from the street outside, 'Put those lights *out*! Blackout! BLACKOUT!' Very quickly, we switch everything off. Luckily, a little dim light from the windows remains. But we haven't got very far exploring Van Tort's Cottage, when suddenly a terrifying unearthly wailing starts up outside and stops us in our tracks.

'Air raid siren,' Simon says. 'It must be on our roof, or the house next door!'

We are standing in the blacked-out downstairs room while this awful noise is going on, and then someone starts knocking on the front door. Ma's Sawbridgeworth friends have come to rescue us, give us food and a bed for the night in their air raid shelter – what a relief! Ma has been delayed, they say, but is arriving very late tonight, and when we wake in the morning there she is with Julyan and Una, Bellman and Billy the cat. She had a bit of an accident on the way which is why she was a day late. Skidded on a wet road and drove the heavily loaded car almost over the edge of a steep escarpment at Yarcombe Hill in Devon. She says there were only three saplings between her and the valley below. She put her hand on the hooter and kept it there, and two men working in a field nearby, who had heard the noise of the crash, came with a tractor and pulled the car back on to the road. But the cat, Billy, had jumped out of the window and she wouldn't go on without him. Anyway, their luggage was all over the place so they had to stay the night with a policeman and his wife. They found Billy after searching the woods in the morning and the policeman helped Ma reload the luggage. Then they drove all day, and arrived here very late last night after we were asleep. And now we have had breakfast and are just about to go up to Van Tort's for an inspection tour in daylight.

Somehow or other we are all together again!

Van Tort's Cottage is Elizabethan, which means it has a straw (thatched) roof, and is a bit higgledy-piggledy. On one side of the living room, stairs almost as steep as a ladder lead up to the first floor, and on the other the front door opens on to the street. The floors are uneven, there are lots of doors and cupboards in odd places, and the kitchen is sort of tacked on like a garden shed at the side. But we all have bedrooms – looking out over a garden at the back with apple trees and a swing. There's only one drawback: the air raid siren. Tonight, after we have gone to bed, it starts up again – and this time it is a proper air raid.

Bellman starts barking and the ack-ack guns clack away as the planes get nearer, then we begin to hear bombs whistling as they come down. Ma is with Julyan, who has woken up because he thinks he is having a nightmare, so Simon and I go into the garden to have a look. A terrific noise from the guns, and we can hear, if not see, the bombers droning round above the clouds of billowing smoke from the tyre factory down near the railway, which is on fire. The light from the fires makes everything – trees, grass, smoke, glass in the windows – bright pink. Simon says he hopes our roof doesn't get a red hot bit of shrapnel on it, as it's only made of hay. Straw, I say – hay, straw, *hay, straw* – then Ma starts yelling at us to come in at once, and we go back inside. It gets a bit quieter, but nobody can sleep. Ma makes us cocoa and we all sit together on the lumpy old sofa in the darkened sitting room while she reads the next chapter of *David Copperfield*. About halfway through the chapter, the all-clear goes, and she snaps the book shut in the middle of a sentence.

'Bedtime,' she says. 'At once!'

Next week it's the new school. Will there be air raids there too?

III
1941–1944
School

I am at the new school now, and Ma visited me today. I showed her the swimming pool and the studio – (two of my drawings are up on the wall), the library, the tennis courts, my room looking out over grass and cedar trees where I sleep with three other girls, the science block, the music school (five rooms with pianos in them), the orchard, and the gymnasium with the roller-skating place on the roof. She liked it all very much (nobody could like it as much as I do, though), but every now and then she said, 'And where do you do lessons?' So in the end I took her into one of the classrooms, and found Ken, our German teacher (my favourite), sitting at a table with two of the boys and a pile of essays, discussing something with them.

'So they do work sometimes?' Ma said to him, laughing.

'Oh yes,' he said. 'Some people work very hard,' and then he smiled and looked at me rather meaningfully (I haven't handed in the German homework he asked me to do this week yet). 'At the moment, I think Marjorie-Ann prefers the swimming pool.'

Do I prefer the swimming pool! Most of the girls think the water is too green and murky, and make a frightful fuss about the cold, but I dive in and swim very fast up to the other end and back all in one go. Then I climb up on to the highest platform, and jump on the long bendy spring board at the bottom with a terrific thump, swoop up into the air with my arms spread out like a bird, before diving into the water. Sometimes, instead of doing a swallow dive, I turn a somersault on the way down. Not many people dare to do this, but I find it easy – I don't know why. And so if anybody is watching I do a somersault or two, suddenly, to surprise them. (Ma would say showing off...)

In lessons, we are divided into sets: brilliant, average, bad, hopeless and so on. For mathematics, for example, there are divisions A, B, C and then D, Marjorie-Ann Watts, hopeless, all by herself. This is because anything to do with numbers, arithmetic, algebra, etc., is a mystery to me, and always has been. I am not exaggerating. I can't remember my tables, can't do division, or add and subtract in my head, can't remember where the point goes, what a fraction or a decimal point is, and so on, however many times I am told. I am used to it, but teachers always think that if they explain very slowly and carefully in a loud voice, I will understand. Or that I am not concentrating, not trying hard enough or not trying at all. I have always been like this, just as I have always been able to draw. (Actually, when I think about it most people can't *draw*. But no one thinks that is peculiar.)

Mr Gimson, the senior mathematics teacher, is giving me special coaching every morning, but I still don't understand what he is talking about, or remember anything he says. I feel quite sorry about it sometimes, and when he comes down to the swimming pool with his stopwatch to time us doing our lengths I put on a special diving display for him, to cheer him up and show him there is one thing I am good at. (Two if you count drawing.)

Lessons I like:

> *English (writing, not grammar)*
> *History*
> *German (because of Ken)*
> *Natural History (because of Geoff)*

89

Art
Games (swimming)
Music (choir)

Don't like:

Everything else
Maths
Algebra
Geometry
Physics
Geography (except drawing maps)
French (Mademoiselle)
Latin
*Domestic Science (things like cooking, and how to iron
    handkerchiefs)*
Religious Studies
Weirdo piano teacher (Bob)
*Outdoor work (awful things like picking frozen Brussels
    sprouts, to help the farm down the road, because all
    their men have been called up)*

There is a choir at this school, boys and girls, and we are singing a cantata by Bach. I have never sung in a choir before, and I am surprised at how much I love it. We are divided into groups – alto, treble, tenor, bass, etc. – each with its own part which you read from a music book as you go along. (I can read music after a fashion because learning the piano and art – and perhaps riding horses – were the only things I liked at my first boarding school.) The separate parts don't sound anything much sung on their own, but when it is all put together and the whole choir is at full stretch, it is stupendous. Harry, the choir master, plays an A on the piano to get the right note, and then we start; part after part joining in and all done with no orchestra or instruments, just voices and singing. Crescendos and fortes are like being in the middle

Grandmother and Mother,
then aged eleven, 1911

Grandmother and
Grandfather the day
he joined the Royal
Army Medical Corps as
a doctor prepared for
'active' service – 1914-18

John Galsworthy with some international writers
at the first PEN congress in 1923

Marjorie Dawson Scott at eighteen, 1918

Lieutenant Commander
Arthur Watts DSO
(in command of ML239,
leader of the smoke screen unit
at Zeebrugge and Ostend,
later Jutland) – 1918

Wedding photograph of
Miss Dawson Scott
and Arthur Watts,
Punch cartoonist, 1925

John Galsworthy, Amy Dawson Scott and Hermon Ould,
the first official secretary of PEN

Aged five months,
with Mother

With Simon and Great Aunt Maude at Fleet

On the Heath with Simon in the pram, Nanny and Rose

Running round the Mill pond at Sea Mills
aged about four or five

Father on Tregoles beach with Leander

'Sister Margaret' – Maggie Furse,
film dress designer

With Father on the Heath, 1935

With Julyan
on the beach – 1937

With Simon and Julyan
at St Mawgan

1940, Uncle Toby in uniform going
to join his regiment next day

Bellman as a puppy

Two keen swimmers

School dance,
aged fifteen

Chelsea School of Art

The Watts family a year of so after moving to Cannon Place – 1947/8

of an ocean storm with sixty-foot waves, a huge wide swell crashing on rocks, but all changing in an instant to calm and quiet where it is marked pianissimo! When it is going on all round you, one part sliding over another and then a change of key suddenly altering everything, something in my heart of hearts, my soul or something, starts flying.

History is good too. In the history room, an enormous chart takes up the whole of one wall. It is divided into segments by straight lines ruled horizontally across it. On the left is the year (1000, 1066, 1542, 1942 or whatever you want). Filling the spaces in the middle are all the important things that have happened in that year. We are doing the Tudors at the moment, and in 1542, for example, Henry VIII was on the throne in England getting ready to chop off poor Queen Catherine Howard's head; there was a war going on between the Turks and the Portuguese, wooden staircases were invented (I love that), and Holbein painted Henry VIII. And it was all going on at *the same time*!

In the space next to the year 1939, Jane, the history teacher, has written 'September, Commencement of World War Two'. And for 1940, 'Germans invade Poland.' 1941 has 'Air battles over Kent' and 1942 is empty of course. If you read back and back through history, there have been wars somewhere in the world *every single year to where the chart begins*! So Simon was right. War just goes on and on all the time, often without one really noticing it. (Unless you are right in the middle, of course.)

It's almost the end of 1941, and the Japanese have gone and bombed a place in America called Pearl Harbour – nothing to do with the Germans. But Ma says it means that President Roosevelt will probably come into the war on our side now, against the Germans.

'So we are not on our own any more,' she says, looking very pleased.

1942

Today is Sunday, and me and my friend Peggy – who is a boarder like me, although her home is so close – are going to walk up through the woods to her parents. They have a house at the top of one of the beech hangers, and a workshop where her father and his apprentices make wooden furniture. His name is Edward, and Peggy says he helped to build the school library.

Everything in Peggy's home is made of wood by her father: the polished elm floors, stairs, doors, candlesticks, picture frames, bookcases, beds, chairs, settle in front of the wood fire, even the door latches. And outside in the lane, there are stacks and piles of wood everywhere; planks of different size and age drying out in a drying shed, split logs small and large, half-sawn trunks of fallen trees, bundles of firewood and hazel sticks, off-cuts, more logs. A sort of wood heaven.

Her parents are completely different to anyone else I've ever met. Tanya, her mother, is half Russian, and an old Russian Aunt Dumdum lives in a sort of thatched two-roomed cottage in the garden and keeps bees. They never lock their front or their side doors, and the sun always seems to be shining up there. They have two COs living with them (Conscientious Objectors, who think fighting is wrong). The COs work on nearby farms, and sometimes they help in the garden. One of them is digging over Dumdum's vegetable patch today. Green lawns slope down towards the edge of the woods, and the garden is a leafy tangle of apple trees and flowers, as well as vegetables, a fruit cage, a fig tree, tomatoes in pots, the beehives and enough strawberries to feed a class full of children.

They don't have a proper lavatory, though. You have to go and sit on a beautiful piece of wood (elm) with a hole in it in an outhouse, just beyond the kitchen door. After you have finished, you shovel earth and wood ash from a bucket into the hole, which has to be emptied from time to time. I think Edward does that, because at lunch today – roast chicken, roast potatoes and peas (all off the ration) – he told me that he keeps it in a heap somewhere in the vegetable garden for a year or two, then feeds it to the strawberries.

'Human dung,' he says. 'Strawberries love it. That's why these are the best strawberries in Hampshire. Have some more, the very first of the season...' Peggy is embarrassed that he is telling me this, but you can't taste the dung, so I hold out my bowl.

'Your friend knows what's good,' he says to Peggy.

Below the house, where the tops of the beech trees crowd up towards the edge of the garden, there is an old juniper tree with a flat top like a platform, and Peggy and I spend hours up there in the sun reading or just doing nothing, gossiping and joking about the boys we are in love with. Last week I was dreaming about Aaron Finzi and Tybalt O'Connor (couldn't decide which I loved best). But I've changed my mind since then – too young, and those silly names! Anyway since yesterday, it's Simon Chan. He is so incredibly handsome – that black Chinese hair – and I have heard him in the music school. Piano. *Brilliant*! Musicians are halfway there as far as I am concerned, and

Peggy says she's the same. Last week she was mad about Peter Harrison, but she's gone off him, because he is only interested in engines, cars, science and things like that. So she's in love with Simon Chan too.

After a couple of hours, we get bored with boys, and grab one of the creepers that hang from the juniper to see who can swing out furthest above the hillside below. We are not supposed to do this, because if the creeper breaks they are afraid we'll fall about half a mile down the hanger and break our necks. But we do it all the same.

Peggy's parents are sitting in deckchairs, talking about the war. So we spend the afternoon up in the juniper tree, and come in to tea at five: hard-boiled eggs (a neighbour has chickens, and they have as many eggs as they want) and salad cream, lettuce from the garden, soda bread made by Peggy's mother, honey and more strawberries. After that, we run down through the woods to 'Jaw' – which is instead of going to chapel or church, and is quite peculiar but not as boring as you might think. This is what happens.

The whole school files into the hall, and if you have got a thing going with one of the boys, you walk in with him and sit together. There is always a lot of whispering and giggling, and craning of heads at the beginning, to see what's changed since last week, who is sitting next to who. I had a week of Micky Sullivan at the beginning of term, but I didn't really like him much; he never said anything, just wanted to hold my hand and walk round and round the cricket pitch. And his breath smelt terrible. Tonight, Simon Chan is not sitting next to anyone, so I stare and stare at the back of his head hoping he'll turn round (he doesn't). Then I see that Peggy is sitting beside *Peter*! I have to laugh, as this afternoon she was saying she never wanted to speak to him again.

After 'Jaw', the girls, accompanied by some of the boys, walk across to the Girls' House – to be in by ten o'clock. Then the boys go up to their rooms and dormitories in the main school building, or that's what's meant to happen. Usually couples wander about together for a while under the trees, and lots of stuff goes on then. One of the senior girls left suddenly last term, and everyone says she left to have a baby because she went 'too far' on the way over to Oakdene, the Girls' House, one evening. Ma has given me terrific lectures about not on any account 'going too far' – i.e. getting pregnant. Quelle disaster, as Mademoiselle would say. Actually, I don't particularly like babies.

Back to 'Jaw'. First, the headmaster gives out any notices, then there is some music. Tonight we had Gervase on his clarinet accompanied by weirdo piano teacher – I think I could fall for Gervase. After that, we all sing. Tonight it's a chorale by someone or other – then there is a talk, i.e. 'Jaw'. It can be anybody – a writer or a poet, an explorer, a musician, a doctor, even a vicar occasionally. We had an Indian poet last week called Rabindreth Tagore, who went on and on until I was almost asleep. They all seem to find something good to say – about human beings usually which, considering how horrible so many of them are, always surprises me! After this, we sing something again, then the headmaster gets up, looks for his lost glasses for the millionth time (on the top of his head), wishes us all a very good evening, and leads the staff up the middle of the hall where they stand waiting in a long line. Then, believe it or not, *every single person in the school files past slowly, to shake their hands and say goodnight!*

The main thing I noticed when I first walked past shaking all those hands was how incredibly different everybody's handshake is. Some are flabby and damp like a piece of wet fish, others crush your fingers together, others just touch your fingers as if you had a contagious disease, others take a long time about it (Mr Gimson for example) and seem not to want to let go. I could hardly believe it was happening the first time, but now I am quite used to it.

The library is like an enormous polished wood barn. There are two floors, a ground floor, and up some stairs, an open gallery arranged round the central well. The bays – each one lined from floor to ceiling with books – have tables where we do our homework. We are all allocated places to sit, and my bay is upstairs and has got the anthropology and geographical books in it. No talking unless it's an emergency, and then only in whispers.

Today, Jane gave me my essay back because the writing was so bad she couldn't read it. So I am meant to be re-writing it. But actually I am up here in my bay on the gallery floor with Peggy and two boys, and we are reading a book which I found on the shelf last week, *The Trobriand Islanders: Sexual Lives of Savages in Melanesia*, by somebody called Malinowski. You wouldn't believe the things he says about these islanders – I do wonder if the librarian has read it, actually. She has just been up telling us off because we are making too much noise. Does she know this book is in her library? (I often look at the other books, not just this one. More interesting than homework.) Silly Monica and her friends were giggling about French kissing the other day. They ought to read this Malinowski.

There is a fair in the village this afternoon and Peggy and me bunked off religious studies to go to it. Half of Form

Two had joined us because of some emergency or other and the room is crammed; people sitting together on the floor, on the sofa, on the tables (religious studies is taught by the headmaster's wife, Mrs M – a sweet gentle lady who never notices anything very much). As it was so crowded and also a lovely sunny day, Peggy and I were sitting on either side of the open window facing the garden, our legs dangling down a foot or two above the grass outside. I look at Peggy and she looks at me and when old Mrs M is waffling on about the meaning of something or other in the Old Testament and has her back turned, we just quietly drop forward and on to the grass.

The fair is small, but we walk about jingling our money and trying everything: helter-skelter, coconut shy, dodgems, carousel, until the only thing left is the rifle range.

'Ere you are my fine young ladies!' the man shouts. 'Shoot poor ole Charlie Chaplin's 'at off and win a lovely prize…'

'I can't shoot,' Peggy says. The man looks at me.

'But you can,' he said, 'I can see it straight away,' and he hands me the rifle. 'Five turns…and if you 'it Charlie's 'at five times you get a prize!'

Of course I have been practising for months and months – years, even – on rabbits, and to cut a long story short I take very careful aim, and do just what he tells me to do. Knock the little black bowler hat down five times. The rifle range man is quite surprised. 'Blimey,' he says. 'You should join the army. I'm out of goldfish… Real silver spoon or a white mouse?'

'White mouse,' I say, thinking it would be made of sugar.

'Take a bit of grub wiv' yer then,' the man says, handing me a small cardboard box and a bag of nuts or seeds or something. 'And make sure you give 'im water. Don't want you coming back saying there's bin a death in the family, do we?'

Which is how at this very moment I have a white mouse with a long pink tail living in my stocking drawer up in H dorm. He is called Albert – Al, for short. My socks and stockings have gone in with Peggy's and I have lined the drawer with newspaper and sawdust I got from the carpentry and woodwork shed. When I asked Geoff in biology what mice live on (I told him I was making a study of mouse habits), he gave me a long list and said he was 'gratified' I was taking an interest in natural history at last.

Al seems as happy as anything and is quite tame. I give him fresh water and food every day, collect cornflakes and breadcrumbs, bits of biscuit or cheese for him to nibble; sometimes I put him in my pocket, and then let him loose on the table in the library for a breather. He likes that, and runs round the table, sniffing at everything, then hides in my pencil box. Today we (the boys in my library bay and me) rigged up a run for him: a tin with both ends knocked out, perched on a pile of books with a ruler leading to another pile of books and another ruler and so on, to form a circle. We soon had him running round and round the table as if he was at a point-to-point. Then Barbara, the librarian came creaking up the stairs, so he had to go back in my pocket.

Bob, my piano teacher, is a real weirdo (looks like an albino crow), and I am tired of remarks like, 'What makes you think you can play the piano if you never practise?' or, 'Why do you play the wrong note when the right one is just next door?' – so I have been going into the music school every day in free time, to play through the Beethoven sonata he has given me to learn. Actually I can play it without the music now, which gives me time to think as I play, instead of worrying about the right notes all the time. (There is a bit in the adagio which makes me feel as if something in my heart is going to burst. Why is something so beautiful so sad?)

Unfortunately, I stayed too long playing Beethoven and was late for French. Mademoiselle kept me back after the class was over, and gave me 'extra werk' to catch up – 'bee-cose I was so bee-ind…'ow would I learn 'eef if I nev-air werked?' Silly cow.

Exams today, which are practice School Certificate papers. Can't do anything much, except write some rubbish in English and history. Maths and algebra I just sit and look out of the window.

I can hardly believe it, but I won the junior fifty-metre freestyle swimming race by two full heads against fifteen other competitors today, and broke the school record! And I was second in the diving competition (I mucked it up because I suddenly noticed Simon Chan staring up at me from one of the spectator benches). Gervase came first with the most beautiful swallow dive I have ever seen. But Mr Gimson, who coaches me in maths, told me I had the best crawl style of anyone he had come across for a very long time, and he was going to put me in the school swimming team and perhaps for the county junior championships.

What shall I do with Albert? It's the summer holidays soon and I can't take him home, the cat or Bellman will get him, and I am not going to put him in the biology lab with the other white mice and the frogs they've got there – I know what they do to them, cruel pigs.

Peggy says I can leave Albert with her, which is just as well because today I found a little nest of chewed-up newspaper bits in a corner of the drawer, and underneath were Albert and three little pink naked mouse babies. All this time, he has been an Albert*ine*!

Ma has got a job as a playgroup organiser, and we are in a new house: Sandy Close, Hertford, Hertfordshire. There is a housekeeper, Pat, and her little girl living with us, to look after us when Ma is at work.

Bellman is very pleased to see me back, and so is Julyan, but I don't remember holidays being as boring as this. Julyan has started the violin. He makes an excruciating noise. Ma says he'll get better – I hope she's right. On Saturday he had a late birthday party, and Ma asked some of his friends from school, mostly girls. All they wanted to do was turn the lights out and run round the house screaming. Afterwards, he said it was the best party he had ever had. (He has never had one before!)

My report came today. The only good comments are for art, music and games/swimming. It starts off all right. Albino Crow says 'a much better term' – does he mean for him or me? Art is: 'Marjorie-Ann shows real talent, and is a pleasure to have in the Art room.' But then history Jane says: 'Capable of good work but Marjorie-Ann lacks concentration and is lazy. She could try a great deal harder.' Mr Gimson burbles on: 'Mathematics is very difficult for this pupil, and we suggest she give up the subject in order to concentrate on those where she needs to catch up.' Ken tries to be nice: 'Marjorie-Ann is an enthusiastic member of the class' – like cleaning the blackboard, or giving him a piece of my birthday cake? Mademoiselle is the worst: 'Until Marjorie-Ann is prepared to work at things she finds difficult, progress is impossible. Her behaviour in class is often disgraceful.' At the end of all this, the headmaster sums up: 'Marjorie-Ann is behind in all subjects – excepting art. We believe she is capable of much better things, and she is going to have to make a real effort to catch up in order to pass her School Certificate in the summer. I hope that next term, she will settle down and take her work more seriously.'

'What's happened?' Ma says. 'Why aren't you working? Aren't you happy at school?'

'Of course I am.'

'Well then?' She waves the report at me.

'I am good at swimming. And...the piano. And drawing.'

'That's not work.'

'Mr Gimson is going to put me in for the swimming team and the junior championships.'

'That's not work either.'

On Sunday, we go for a walk on the boring dreary common. Simon is in one of his silent furies because, he says, Julyan has pushed in front of him at the gate and broken the model aeroplane he had just finished constructing, and was going to try out on the common this afternoon. Julyan is nagging on and on about how he *didn't* knock into Simon, he dropped it himself, so it isn't his FAULT is it? *IS IT?* And Ma is looking so sad and worried I want to scream, and am

101

wishing I was back at school with Peggy eating strawberries or swinging out above the treetops in the sunshine. Only Bellman is happy, rushing about looking for rabbits (there aren't any). It starts to rain, and we all get soaking wet.

After tea, can you believe it, Ma makes me sit down and do French revision! Then she makes Julyan practise his violin. Of course he does it right in my ear, which gives me a headache.

There is a garden at the back of number six, and on the other side of a six-foot fence, a not-much-used path leads from the high street to the playing fields. It is almost grown over with brambles and long grass, but sometimes people take short cuts along there, walk their dogs.

Today, I was out in the garden with Bellman, and I heard some moaning and groaning, and heavy sighs – like a cow fallen over and unable to get up – coming from the other side of the fence. I couldn't think what it was. The fence is made of wood, and just to the right near my knees I could see a large knothole. So I bent down and had a look. On the other side just off the path, a soldier was lying in the long grass on top of a girl. He was in his khaki uniform, and she had her arms round him, and kept trying to pull her skirt down but I could see her white skin and her suspenders, and quite a lot of the top of her flopping about. The back of the soldier's head was visible, but hers was hidden in the long grass. I watched them for quite a long time heaving about and sighing and panting; it looked very uncomfortable. Simon and Julyan came to have a look, but then Bellman started barking like a maniac, trying to scratch and dig up the fence. The next time I squinted through the hole, they were sitting up and combing their hair.

'What have you been doing out there?' Pat asked when we went in to tea.

'Nothing,' we all said at once, laughing our heads off.

The Germans have attacked Stalingrad and there is a terrible fight going on there, even though the Russians are starving. I *hate* the Germans.

This afternoon, Simon and I have to take his *Aircraft Recognition* book back to the library. On the way home we go the long way round; up through the woods above the town, and then along the edge of some cornfields.

It is a scorching hot day, blue sky and corn golden brown in the sun. I can hear a woodpecker hammering as we dawdle along the path picking blackberries. From up here the sky looks huge, like a painting, and there is a view right across Hertford town, the gasworks, spires of the churches, little red-brick houses, fields and woods beyond. As we stand there eating blackberries and looking down at the town, we hear the noise of aeroplane engines zooming and whining.

'Dogfight,' Simon says, craning his head back. Sure enough, very high above us and so small they look almost like toys, silver planes are scribbling spidery black trails on the empty blue. Skeins of vapour float behind them.

'Hurricanes…chasing Heinkels,' Simon says, turning his head as, from behind the hill, comes the drone of approaching bombers. 'Who are escorting… Messerschmitts going home. Probably.' We gaze up at the black swastikas as they roar overhead.

A Hurricane streaks past, guns rattling. In slow motion, one of the bombers begins to tip down towards the patchwork of fields and woods beneath us, smoke trailing.

It seems like ages while we wait, but then the ground shakes suddenly, and seconds later we hear the bang. Two more Hurricanes chase after the German bombers grinding towards the horizon. As we watch, another Messerschmitt wobbles, tips, begins to lose height and in the distance, explodes in mid-air, bits spinning in all directions. The others fly on and are soon out of sight. Everything is quiet again. Just the woodpecker and the clock on the bluecoat school tower striking four.

'I bet there's a lot of stuff in that Messerschmitt,' Simon says, shading his eyes to gaze at the field where the first plane came down and smoke is now billowing. He means all the instruments and gear he and his *Aircraft Recognition* friends might be able to strip out from the crashed plane once the Home Guard have been in to collect the bodies and live ammunition. When he's at school and on their free afternoons, Simon and co bicycle off to descend like jackals on any plane carcase they can find, rummaging about to unscrew and remove the most amazing stuff – magnetic compasses, lamps, dials, altimeters, intercom microphones, yards of cable, even a box of hand grenades once (those were handed in). They take away everything they can carry on bicycles. His room is full of it.

'How far is that field?' he asks dreamily.

'Miles. Too far.'

'Might be worth having a look?'

'Not *now*, it's still burning. We'll be late for tea…come on.'

When it rains, instead of games we have something here called 'Wet Run'. You put on shorts and a shirt and run, in the rain, out of the school gates along the road for quarter of a mile, up towards Stonor Hill and the woods, down a muddy lane past the Horder estate, right, then left and on, to back where you started but sopping wet. Seniors tick you off as you pass certain landmarks. It's not as bad as it sounds, because after a shower you are allowed to use any time over as you like. So I always whizz round like a bullet, and then go to the studio, or find a free piano in the music school.

Today Mr Gimson is standing in his mac under a black umbrella with his stop watch, timing us all as we splash past. (He's got timing on the brain!) After tea he asks to see me. 'I have timed you several times now, Marjorie-Ann, and I am impressed. Your speeds are consistently excellent. Have you thought of taking up running?' To me, running fast is just a way of getting from A to B as quickly as possible. Boring. So I say I'll stick to swimming, thanks. He seems quite disappointed.

Before I came to this school, I had never seen a lot of naked girls larking about in a shower together. But mud-splashed and soaked through after Wet Run, we are all desperate for a shower when we get back to Oakdene, so it's a beeline for the shower rooms. Dressed, girls look much like…well, other girls. But naked in the shower, it is surprising how extremely different they all are, one from another. Pam, for example – so small and plump and womanly with her neat triangle of black hair, or Bridget, flat and muscular, hairless; or beanpole Christina, with her ginger fuzz and skinny body; roly-poly Lucy, huge flabby stomach and thighs quivering – all animatedly chatting, water and spray cascading in streams from their various shiny slippery bodies. The strangest one is Corinna, who has a tiny small-hipped little body topped by outsize full

105

breasts hanging down above her stomach. Sometimes, I can hardly bear to look at her she seems such a freak. But out of the shower and dressed, she looks quite normal.

There is a dance at school tonight, and I am going to wear my new red dress. Pat, who lives with us in Hertford, made it for me to wear at weekends – when we are allowed to wear our own clothes. (I've even curled up my hair a bit, like she showed me.)

The dining room has been cleared, and Ken is doing the music – a record player in the corner. Peggy didn't want to come at first, but I have never been to a dance so I persuaded her. Very soon I wish I hadn't. As soon as the music starts, people begin to dance, and quite quickly she goes wafting off with Peter. Worse, Simon Chan walks past me with Barbara Capelli from Form One, and leads her away into the crowd. I am left on my own, everyone looking at me in my stupid dress and laughing because it is so awful to be left standing on the edge with people like Judy and Monica who are fat and silly and nobody likes. I am just about in tears with pretending I'm fine when I am not, when Johan Petersen, one of the very senior boys, comes up and asks me to dance. I know that he is the best dancer in the school, so I don't know what to do.

'I've never danced with anybody before,' I say as he leads me out on to the floor.

'Relax,' he says, smiling his Clark Gable smile, 'you'll be fine.' He lifts one foot and points it at the ground. 'Like this, look! Follow me... *STEP*, *one*, two-three, *STEP*, *one*, two-three...it is a *waltz*!'

I know what a waltz is, three beats in a bar, and I step out, first on to my right foot, then on the left, then on the right and...suddenly, I am dancing! As if I have done it all my life, circling the hall exactly in time to the beat of the music. Johan grips me (like iron), and swings me round faster and faster, the skirt of my red dress flaring out and everyone looking at us and clapping. Johan is smiling at me – I've never stared back into a boy's eyes like this before, but it's all part of the dance and I laugh and smile at him, knowing that I *can* dance, that it's me he's chosen, that he is the most handsome boy in the room, more handsome even than Simon Chan, and that we are spinning round together for ever and ever – or anyway until the music stops which, in due course, it does.

'Very, very good,' he says, holding me at arm's length as if he is considering what to do with me next. 'Now is foxtrot…you know?' (Johan comes from Denmark, sent here because of the war and his English is not very good.) 'Like so? Follow…me.'

Foxtrots are different from waltzes. You shuffle round the room clasped together cheek to cheek like a damp jam sandwich. *SLOW…SLOW…*step-step slow – and so on. Everyone else is squashed together too – which is all right for them – but I am not sure I like being pressed up so close that you can feel someone else's shirt buttons, their strange hard body, smell their sweat. Johan seems to like it a lot, though. He has slowed up so much that we are practically standing still just rocking while he squeezes the breath out of me with his iron arms. (I am a bit embarrassed about how I can feel absolutely all of him though my thin dress.) When the music stops, he says it is so hot – wouldn't it be nice to go out on the terrace and under the trees for a stroll? I know what that means, and it's so exciting that he wants to take me with him out there, but quite alarming as well. So I just dither and laugh and don't really answer.

'Yes, well…um…I am OK…er…' We stand together for a minute grinning like idiots, then the music starts up again and Jimmy Grant comes prancing up wanting to dance. Off I go with Jimmy, but out of the corner of my eye I can see Johan watching me. Then he's dancing again too, whirling round with one of the senior girls, and all I want is to be dancing with him in his iron arms instead of Jimmy – who keeps treading on my feet.

I got shouted at by Mademoiselle today. She kept me back after the lesson and said I hadn't taken enough 'troubelle' with my French homework.

'Do 'eet again,' she says. 'You are capable of much bettaire – and look at me pleeeze, when I speak to you?' (I am watching some squirrels running up and down the beech tree outside the window.) 'Enfin! What 'ave you in your pockette?'

This is awkward. Peggy has given me back one of Albertine's babies, and I had brought him or her into school for an outing in the library.

'Pocket? Nothing…'

'Alors, let me see…*immediatement*!' She is working herself into a rage, so I fish about and bring out Albert/Albertine junior. Mademoiselle gives a little scream and backs away. 'Mon Dieu! A mouse! In your…leave the room! You keep a *mouse*?'

'He's quite friendly–'

'*In-su-por-table!* The headmaster will 'ear about this. Leave! Leave the room.'

Which is why, I suppose, the headmaster has asked to see me – and I am waiting outside his office now, twiddling my thumbs.

Peggy says I don't look much like a caterpillar even though I am trying to turn over a new leaf! The long and the short of the headmaster's interview is that I have poor marks in almost every subject except art, which I am good at because there I actually do some work. French is particularly bad, he says, but I am very behind in everything else as well, and make no effort to catch up. I am rude and undisciplined and, if I don't pull up my socks and start to take school work seriously, I might as well leave. Because it is a waste of everybody's time continuing to try and teach me.

'We know you are capable, Marjorie-Ann. But you are in Form Two now, you have to work. Do you understand?' (What could I say? I don't want to leave.) 'You have already dropped maths, but there is no reason why you cannot do well in all other subjects…if you work. It is your choice. You are taking School Certificate next summer, and I want a big improvement by the end of this term, otherwise I see little point in you remaining with us. I will speak to you again when I have read your end of term report and discussed it with other members of staff.'

A bit of a nasty shock, although there was no mention of Mademoiselle – except, as I was leaving the room, he gave a little smile and said that I must make sure that my pets, if I have any, are always kept in the pet enclosure. (Peggy has a tame rabbit in a hutch there.)

I walked round the orchard several times feeling very uncomfortable. I definitely do not want to leave.

Another nasty surprise this morning. Just when I was getting used to Sandy Close, Ma writes that we are moving again – back to London. (The Blitz is more or less over.) Ma has got another job – more money she says in her letter. Not back to our old house, but a flat, very small, in Belsize Park, one Tube stop away from Hampstead. She and Julyan are moving there next week. He will go to a day school, and Simon and I will join them at the beginning of the Christmas holidays. She doesn't say anything about Pat, but I hope she is coming with us.

Christmas holidays, and Uncle Toby – who is still in the army, but attached to the War Office in London now – is taking me to a concert at the Albert Hall today. I wore my red dress and 'borrowed' Ma's silk stockings. (It's not stealing because I'm going to put them back.) A pianist called Myra Hess – famous, he says – is playing Tchaikovsky. I didn't know an orchestra and piano together can sound like this: brave and glorious, beautiful, sad all at the same time. Uncle Toby said he feels the same. In the Underground going home, people are sleeping on the platforms.

Ma and I have a row about her stockings.

'*I* don't have any silk stockings!' I say.

'That doesn't mean you should *steal* mine. Trudy Bliss sent them to me from America. They are my last pair.'

'But I don't have any clothes coupons *left*!'

'Save up then, like everybody else.'

I really hate my mother sometimes.

The flat in Belsize Park is on the first floor, small and dingy, gloomy because of all the sticky tape on the windows, but it has four bedrooms and an Anderson shelter smelling of tomcat down in the garden. Also a peculiar ramshackle lift attached to the wall outside the kitchen. I don't know what this is for. Rubbish? Coal? (Julyan wants to get in it and try it out, but I don't think it looks all that safe.) My bedroom is off the kitchen – more of a cupboard than a bedroom it is so small – and Simon and Julyan are sharing, which doesn't work as they fight all the time. Then there's a sitting room, and Ma's bedroom, and another room for Ma's new help, Edna.

Simon has made a friend, a boy of his age who lives on the other side of the road in one of the flats directly opposite. Last week they fixed up a bit of Meccano that travels across the street along an electrified wire they have strung up balcony to balcony, and then back again. It works off the train set transformer apparently, '20 volts DC' – whatever that means.

Electricity is a big draw, but it is gunpowder and explosives that are Simon's real interest in life. He has just got hold of a miniature cannon that can fire ball bearings – scrounged from an old bike he and his friend found on a dump somewhere; the gunpowder is made from some shotgun shells taken to bits. They sit on the balcony together firing this cannon, and you can hear the ball bearings 'pinging' on the windows opposite. Yesterday an old lady came out from one of the downstairs flats after her window had been 'pinged' several times and looked around, but of course she couldn't see anything. Higgins, the porter-caretaker man who looks after all the flats in this street, hasn't noticed the electrified wire or heard the 'pinging' yet. But he probably will.

Housekeeper Pat didn't want to leave Hertford, so we have got Edna now. She is meant to help when Ma is at work, look after Julyan when he gets back from school and get him to practise. Not easy, as Julyan runs rings round everybody and has his own ideas about how he spends his time (by the way, his violin playing is definitely improving, I suppose because he does practise occasionally nowadays).

Edna is pathetic. Looks like some sort of dilapidated ostrich in a blue overall. Definitely a bit wanting.

'Upper stories closed for the duration,' Simon says, tapping his head.

'A few steps short of a staircase,' I say and we both fall about laughing – and get a lecture from Ma about good manners and making people feel at home. Actually, if Edna's in the mood she can be quite sparky.

Simon and his friend got bored with the Meccano thing and have rigged up a rough kind of telephone as well now, which means more wires stretching from balcony to balcony. It is quite good; you can hear people sort of screeching in the distance (although that turned out to be the couple in the next-door flat having a row). Unfortunately, Higgins saw it today and is furious, he came up to see Ma, who was still at work. We were all standing behind the door listening, and I must say Edna did pretty well.

'Is that there wire contraption hanging from the balcony anything to do with number sixty-five?' he shouts the moment Edna opens the door.

'What if it is?'

'Take it down in double quick time, or…'

'Or what?'

'I'll give someone what for! Those boys–'

'No need to shout, Higgins,' says Edna.

'Don't you 'iggins me. Those boys are out of control…'

'What boys?'

'I'm going to report them!'

'Report what you like *Mister* Higgins,' says Edna very hoity-toity, and shuts the door grinning. Opens it again a crack and says. 'Anyway, it ain't got nothing to do with me, and Mrs Watts is not at home your lordship!'

So poor Ma had 'Mister' Higgins waiting for her when she got back from work, as well as Edna complaining about Julyan.

'Mrs Watts! I want to speak to you!'

'Yes Edna, what about?'

'Julyan threw the fish at me...'

'That was wrong of him.'

'...then he ran away!'

'Where is the fish now?'

'In the dustbin.'

'Oh *Edna!* That was supper!'

A few minutes later, in comes Julyan holding the, by now, definitely smelly fish. 'Here you are!' he says. 'I went down to the dustbin and got it back for you!'

Simon was given a chemistry set for Christmas with a Bunsen burner, test tubes, iron filings and little jars of chemicals, with which he has been conducting experiments. The jars have got labels stuck on them telling you what's inside: strontium is red, copper sulphate green, and there is a yellow one, I can't remember what that is. He mixes up different powders and chemicals, and sometimes makes the most amazingly beautiful colours (which usually smell dreadful).

Today he has been in the kitchen messing about all morning making gunpowder, which smells pretty bad. There is a knock on our front door, and Higgins stands there.

'I have had complaints about a gas leak...coming from number sixty-five,' he says. 'Where is your mother?'

'At work,' we say.

'I'll have a look,' and in he marches.

Luckily, Simon has put all the chemical bits and pieces away, leaving only the Bunsen burner and the saucepan.

113

And the smell. Higgins has a good sniff round, and then spends a long time examining the gas cooker and the pipes, twiddling the taps and turning them on and off.

'Can't find nothing wrong with the gas,' he says. 'But there's a funny smell in this flat. What you got in that there saucepan young man?'

'Powdered saltpetre, charcoal…'

Higgins glares at the twists of charred newspaper. Matches are almost impossible to get hold of nowadays, so we use a gadget with a flint in it that makes a spark, and light things with that.

'You know what happens to children what plays with matches, don't you?'

'Actually, I have run out of matches,' Simon says, 'could you lend me some?'

'I'm not lending you nothing!' Higgins says. 'And tell your ma I want to speak to her when she gets home!'

When he has gone, Simon picks up the saucepan and the gas lighter gadget. 'Perhaps I'll try mixing it wet this time,' he says.

The holidays go on like they usually do. Simon fiddling with his chemistry set, Julyan arguing with Edna about how long he should practise, me writing and illustrating a long story about some magic dolphins – then my report drops through the letter box: *Marjorie-Ann Watts, Autumn Term 1942.* Jane writes: 'A better term, although her written work needs much more effort. She has a good appreciation of history, and could do well.' English is not too bad either: 'A good grasp of the subject and she can work well when interested. She should understand, however, that written work does not require illustration.' I will pass over Mademoiselle's comments and go straight on

114

to art, which is good. Mr Gimson is nice too. He says that I am 'a natural athlete', and that I am 'a valued member of the swimming team' and, wait for it, 'her prowess on the games field and in athletics generally is greatly to be admired. A very good term on this score'. (Nothing about leaving.)

Ma says, 'Fine if you are planning to be a games mistress or a PT instructor. On the other hand, unless you pass School Certificate somehow, it's a secretarial course next.'

1943

It is warm and sunny today, so we are going up to see a friend of Ma's in Hampstead. She is living in the basement of her large house on the edge of the Heath, because the RAF are using the rest of it for offices. On the way home we walk back across the Heath. There are anti-aircraft guns positioned right across the piece of land that slopes down from East Heath Road to the ponds, grey barrage balloons strung out above. The soldiers – gunners in tin hats and khaki uniforms – have dug little shallow pits where they have their anti-aircraft guns hidden under dark green netting with leaves and grass on top. Camouflage. They are very friendly, and call out, inviting us to have a cup of tea. Ma talks to one of them, and discovers he has only just joined up and comes from Truro in Cornwall. I am glad they are there. The Blitz is over (there haven't been any raids for a long time); but when I look up at the sky nowadays, it is not friendly like it used to be. I hope we bomb Jerry to pieces.

Everywhere you go in London, you see GIs, American soldiers. They smoke cigars, are amazingly well dressed and good-looking, but cheeky. Always calling out things like: 'Hey there! What's cookin' good lookin'?' or, 'Going my way, babe?' Ma says I have got to be extremely careful however friendly they are, and never on any account go off alone with any of them. But I think she is exaggerating.

Last term, Ma wrote to me and said that she was going to arrange German coaching for me in the holidays! I wasn't exactly pleased, but actually I quite like Mr Reif – Luli. He and Mrs Reif and their two daughters live in a crescent off England's Lane, and are refugees. He had a bookshop in Berlin and loves books more than anything. He listens to me reading to him out of a German newspaper – where does he get that from? – then we have 'German conversation', although he does most of the conversing! He is a member of the British Communist Party, thinks everything in Russia is perfect, and is always telling me about it; all in German, of course.

Today, after we had finished, he was talking about how he would like to go and live in Russia. 'It's a wonderful country... No one is poor in Russia, and there is plenty of food. Everyone is equal. Working men are heroes there – look at how they are fighting!' I am not sure what he is talking about, but Mrs Reif appears at that moment and says, 'Don't listen to his nonsense. Would you like a cup of tea?'

For next week, he's asked me to write him a letter, in German, about my school – and, yes, I can illustrate it.

We are sitting round the gas fire in the little sitting room of the flat and Ma is getting near the end of *Oliver Twist*.

Yesterday Bill Sykes murdered poor Nancy, and tonight I suppose it will be what happens to him, the wicked so-and-so. Serve him right, whatever it is.

As usual, the boys are fidgeting and messing about – Julyan with his Dinky tractor, and Simon with bits of string and a box of matches – where did he get those from? There are none in the hardware shop... – down near the fire surround. Ma is just beginning to read the bit where the mob has started to chase Sykes through the streets, when I notice that there is a piece of string alight, fizzling slowly towards the gas fire.

'What's that?' I say, pointing. 'There's a funny smell.'

'A fuse,' Simon says very quietly. Ma looks up from Dickens, and sees the string smoking and sparking along on the tiles.

'Is that gunpowder, Simon?'

'Well...yes...' Ma gets up and stamps hard on the string. 'I only wanted to see what would happen when it reached the fire!' He sounds surprised.

'Have you got any more? Any gunpowder left, anywhere?'

'Um...well...'

'Bring it here immediately!' Ma is fed up with this sort of thing. He melted some lead soldiers in her milk saucepan the other day, and when she came to make toast in the morning, the grill dripped bits of lead into the toast. The saucepan was ruined of course. So was the toast – I don't know how many points on the ration cards wasted.

Simon comes back with quite a sizeable amount of gunpowder mixed up in a tea cup, a silver teaspoon half full of solidified lead soldered into it, four boxes of matches, some wax tapers and a ball of string. She puts the gunpowder down the lavatory, tells him off about the teaspoon and confiscates the rest. Then we all sit down again, and Ma goes on reading. A quarter of an hour later Sykes comes to his terrible end, and even the boys are sitting bolt upright, listening! Old Dickens can certainly tell a good story!

Back at school, my marks are better – which they should be, because I am definitely working harder than I ever have before. For School Certificate, I am taking art, history, English, German, French, and geography, but not Latin. Not having either maths or Latin means I cannot sit the university entrance exams, but that doesn't matter, as I am going to art school – or that's what Ma says.

'You are going to have to earn your living somehow,' she says. 'And art is your best option out of that lot.' I would rather just sit and play the piano, actually, but I know Ma would say that isn't a job, so I keep quiet.

Today I am writing a letter to Luli – mostly illustration. Actually, when I think about it, why am I trying to learn German so hard? They are our enemies – *everybody's* enemies. Then I remember Beethoven and Bach – they were German – and Luli, who is or was a German. In his letter to me – in German, of course – he says that the Russians are winning everywhere, what a wonderful country Russia is…

More good news when we get into the history room today: Jane tells us that German troops, ninety thousand of them, have surrendered to the Red Army at Stalingrad. We all cheer. Then, at the weekend, Peggy says that she heard from her aunt – who has been staying with them – that there have been some more air raids on London, and the barrage was the fiercest her aunt had ever heard. I thought of the soldiers cleaning their guns on the grass above the ponds, and then suddenly about Ma and Julyan, and Edna (Simon is away at school like me). I told Peggy what I was thinking, and she said if anything happened I could go and live with them.

Time is going so quickly it's almost the holidays again. We are all working like slaves. No more mucking around, and actually I am beginning to enjoy French. (Mademoiselle has been seen out in the town, walking about arm in arm with a Free French officer!) And some of the work is quite interesting – English, for example. Also in German, Ken said he was really amazed at the 'strides' I have made because of my hard work.

Portsmouth is getting bombed. We can hear the guns at night. It's because it's a port and has Royal Navy vessels docked there. We had an 'Air Raid Alert' at school last night. Getting up just after we had gone to bed, and traipsing down to the shelter.

Apart from a tremendous fuss when Higgins, the porter, caught Julyan and a friend hauling each other up and down in the little outside lift at the Mansions, I can't remember what we did in the holidays. But now it's past the middle of the summer term, and School Certificate papers are in two weeks time. After that it is sports day, and Ma is coming to watch me swim. She has never seen me racing or in the team here, doing my diving. And there are some of my drawings and paintings up on the studio walls at the moment.

I got a better report at Easter. Ken is very pleased. 'An excellent term. M.A. has been working consistently hard.' And Mademoiselle, whose comments are written in purple ink in a large slanting hand all loops and flourishes, says she has noticed an astonishing improvement, and she too is very 'pleased'. (Mademoiselle is engaged to the Free French officer, and is wearing an engagement ring with a diamond the size of a pigeon's egg.)

Exams are finished. Awful. I am sure I have failed geography, and French. And probably German.

We have been battling through the preliminary swimming heats, every yard timed by Mr Gimson, and now the freestyle race is between me, Imogen Potter and Barbara Capelli. (Mr Gimson thinks I can break my own record.) I have been practising my underwater racing 'turnarounds', and at the moment I am faster than anyone else! In the diving competitions I am down for the 'double pike and half twist', 'back flip' and a 'one and a half'. Hope I can do it. Only Gervase is better than me at the double pike.

Ma couldn't come to sports day. Julyan was ill with measles, and she didn't want to leave him with dimwit Edna. I won the freestyle race and broke my own record. And Gervase and I tied for the diving competition. Mr Gimson was very pleased and came up and shook my hand, and said well done, a first rate performance. But I am sad because I wanted Ma there to watch me.

In the holidays we are going down to Itchenor. Ma has still got her little dinghy *Curlew* in someone's back garden there, and we are going sailing. Father's big boat is there too, but it has been lying out in a field since the war started, and needs repairing.

I have only just discovered that Bellman is no longer here. Last term while I was in the middle of exams at school, Ma went and gave him away! To some horrible family in the country!

She says that when he was left on his own in the flat, which he had to be quite a lot, he barked and howled and the neighbours had complained. As had Higgins, the porter. So she had found a really nice family with children in the country, who would love him and take him for walks.

'But *I* love him!'

'You are not here.'

'You should have asked me–'

'You were at school. Besides, I know what you would have said.'

'I hate you!'

'That doesn't help anybody.'

'Where is he?'

'In the country.'

On and on we go arguing. He would be much happier in the country, it was a nice family, it was not fair to keep an active creature like a spaniel alone in a small flat, I was being selfish…etc., etc.

'How do I know he's all right?

'We will go and visit him, to make sure.'

'When?'

'Soon.'

'I *hate* you!'

Itchenor turned out to be the worst summer holiday I can remember. First Bellman wasn't there. Then we were in a bell tent in somebody's field, and there was a detachment of soldiers billeted in tents on the other side of the hedge shouting and clapping and bellowing raucous songs until after midnight every night. It rained, and Simon got mumps. Simon is always more ill than anyone else with these things, and on about the third night when he was really bad, into a gap between songs, Ma shouted: 'Will you please, PLEASE be quiet. I have a very sick child in my tent over here!' There was instant silence, and in the morning the sergeant brought round a huge bunch of grapes and some Robinson's Barley Water, and asked whether they could help in any way. She thanked him and his men very much but she was all right, we were all right, and when he was better, Simon, with his face like a melon because of the mumps, visited the camp – and the soldiers showed him all their weapons and ammunition. Real explosives; ordnance, it's called. He was very, very pleased. (I hope they didn't tell him how it is made.)

I got my exam results today, and have surprised everyone, including myself. Five credits – art and written English were best. As, distinctions in both. And everything else except geography is As too! I'm amazed. So is Ma, and she keeps hugging me and saying, 'I knew you could do it, my clever daughter.'

The British Army has landed in mainland Italy, and I think the Americans are there too. In any case, London is full of GIs! Wherever you go there are crowds of them hanging about. They look so different from the little cock sparrow English Tommies. Much bigger and so smartly dressed. Well-cut uniforms made from really good cloth, not the rough khaki that our soldiers wear. They have lots of money, smoke cigars and take taxis everywhere!

Round the corner from us in Belsize Park, there is a large official-looking brick building which houses a lot of the Wrens working in London. So a few GIs are always hanging around there after dark hoping to pick one up.

As a reward for my School Certificate results, Uncle Toby is taking me to the National Gallery to a lunchtime concert today – Myra Hess again. I am meeting him in the foyer of the Piccadilly Hotel which is near his office, and no sooner have I got through the revolving doors than a tall smiling GI comes over to me.

'Why *hello* beautiful!...I'm Glen. What's your name, honey?' He has a lovely soft drawling kind of voice. Another one joins him, both of them very tall and very friendly. 'Hi there!' they drawl. 'C'mon honey, let's have a good time...'

'I am waiting for my uncle,' I say. They are both amazingly good-looking, like film stars. Tanned, smiling, handsome faces. I am going to say 'I am not allowed to go off with any GIs' when Uncle Toby pushes through the doors.

'This young lady is with me,' he says, looking extremely stern, and grasping my arm. He is in his major's uniform but looks like a midget next to them.

'Yeah, yeah...the uncle...' They are roaring with laughter, rolling their eyes and winking at me. Obviously they don't believe him.

'Over paid, over sexed and over here,' Uncle Toby mutters as we go out through the revolving doors.

It's a bright sunny day, the grey barrage balloons above Trafalgar Square catching the light as they pull at their mooring hawsers in the breeze. The air raid siren goes as we walk towards the National Gallery, which is a surprise – I haven't heard it for a long time. But nothing more happens, for a while. In the National Gallery, only one picture is on display – the others have been taken away and stored in a safe place.

Myra Hess is playing a Beethoven sonata, number one hundred and eleven. (I have been trying to play some of the slower bits, but most of it is much too difficult for me.) Halfway through, we hear anti-aircraft guns starting up.

Towards the end of the sonata, at about bar one hundred and seventy-four, the right hand has a slow descending scale in C major from high C in groups of nine per beat. So, three times C to B, each an octave lower, ending in a B. Right in the middle of this we all hear the whistle of a bomb. Myra Hess does not hesitate for a single instant – continues on down as if nothing else in the world exists except the music. On the bus home I say to Uncle Toby: 'That bomb, in the Beethoven, it didn't explode? There was no crash?'

'Such is the power of music,' he replies.

Yesterday I heard Julyan playing a Mozart gavotte piece with his teacher Tamara Osborn (Julyan calls her 'Tomorrow'), a pianist who teaches at his school. I was quite surprised. He stands there reading from what's propped on a stand in front of him as if he knows what he is doing, and it sounded…well, like music. The piano helps, of course.

Julyan likes his school. It is co-ed and supposed to be 'progressive', according to Ma. Boys and girls, and a lot of music and painting – he's even done some cooking! I am not sure about real lessons, though – whether he does any, I mean. They always seem to be out in the grounds lighting fires or climbing trees.

He came home yesterday with some incredible story that the headmaster (who has a wife), and the biology teacher (Julyan only knows her Christian name but she definitely doesn't have a husband), are having a baby together. I asked Ma about it and she said what nonsense! She knew the headmaster and his wife very well, and Julyan must have got the wrong end of the stick – or the child he heard it from was making it up.

Two days later, when she saw one of the other mothers, she found out it was true. All the children are talking about it. I told Simon, and he said, 'Well, that's biology for you!' Apparently the other mother thinks it is shocking, and is taking her child away from the school.

Churchill and Roosevelt and Uncle Joe (Stalin) are going to meet and talk about the Second Front. Everybody knows it is coming, but not when or where. Meantime, the Allies are fighting their way up through Italy and raids over Germany are increasing: Hamburg, Dresden, last night Bremen and Ems, Stuttgart. If it stops them bombing us, I'm glad. Particularly after what happens on my journey back to school for my last term.

There have been very few air raids on London recently, but last night a small bomb wrecked the entrance to Belsize Park station and it was closed this morning. Ma had to go to work and I said I would be perfectly OK to get myself off on my own, so this afternoon I had to get to Victoria to catch my train back to school.

The siren went as I walked down to Chalk Farm, and when finally I got to Victoria things were chaotic as a bomb had fallen somewhere on one of the buildings at the back of the station, and everything was disrupted. Nobody seemed to know anything, but after a lot of waiting around, enquiries, etc., I was told to take a much later train, on a different line, to a different destination, and to change en route.

Victoria was awful. A smell of brick dust and gas in the air and, although I couldn't see any actual bomb damage, crowds of milling people, military police, ARP squads, drunken Scottish ratings on their way back to Portsmouth hanging out of windows of the train I was meant to be getting on. They were shouting and singing and got particularly noisy when they saw me; grabbed my suitcase and wouldn't give it back unless I got into the train with them. In the end, Mr Brown – a First World War army sergeant, it seems – blasted them with a lot of blistering language, rescued my case, and pulled me up into his compartment to sit with him and his wife.

The train stopped even before it reached Clapham Junction. It was blacked out of course, but searchlights twitching backwards and forwards and the sporadic flicker of gunfire gave us a ghostly light of sorts. We waited and waited, and after what seemed like hours and to the shouts and cheers of the ratings, were finally shunted off into a siding somewhere. Incendiaries had been dropped along this bit of the line earlier, causing small fires beside the tracks, and we could make out several other passenger trains silhouetted against the pale sky, waiting like us. A long, darkened troop train rattled through, and then another. Ahead of them, coastal guns kept up a dull irregular thumping.

'Portsmouth's copping it tonight,' ex-sergeant Brown muttered.

'I thought you said the Blitz was over?' Mrs Brown made it sound as if the war were his fault.

I don't know how long we stayed there. Mrs Brown had cashed her sweet ration earlier that day and gave me a big piece of chocolate, but I wasn't really hungry. We sat listening to the anti-aircraft fire (deafening), ambulance sirens, occasional explosions. Then the all clear went. The ratings – quieter during the last hour – began cheering, but the train remained where it was. At last, a railway man appeared with a torch, his face blackened by smoke and soot. 'Any civilians in here? Where are you trying to get to Miss?' And when I told him, 'You won't get through on this line tonight. Jerry's left us with half a dozen big craters up ahead. Follow me, and we'll see if we can get you on the Eastbourne train.'

Leaving the ratings behind still shouting and singing, the Browns – Sergeant Brown carrying my case – me, and a few others, climbed down and walked back along the track.

The glowing fires, railway lines gleaming silvery pink in the dark, evening star hanging like a silver witch ball over black chimney pots, made it look like a scene from a painting by Hieronymus Bosch (I wrote an essay on him last term).

'They dropped flares along here,' the railway man said. 'Like daylight, it was.'

It certainly wasn't like daylight now. We followed along behind, stumbling over lines and sleepers, until we reached some blacked-out carriages in another siding. An engine was shunted into position, and after a long wait we pulled away, jolting and rocking over the points. The Browns got off at Guildford, and I reached my station at a quarter to three! The first person I saw on the platform was Mademoiselle.

'Mon Dieu, quelle horreur!' she cried. 'Ma pauvre enfant… Alors, un tax-ee, we must 'ave un tax-ee, non?'

There were no taxis, of course, but she made such a fuss that a volunteer was found to drive us up to the school.

I never thought I could be so pleased to see Mademoiselle! She had been to visit her fiancé, passing through London before he rejoined his squadron. They are getting married the next time he is on leave, but 'Enfin, when will that be? When will this terrible war end?' She was praying night and day for the moment when she and Antoine could return to France, back to his lovely garage in Limoges and 'be 'appy for evaire'. I quite liked Mademoiselle by the time we drove through the school gates.

The first two days of term are spent discussing exams and who got what. Everyone is in a good mood – except silly Monica, who has to retake three papers!

Jane said my history papers were solid and convincing, and showed I had 'thought about the subject in a serious way'. 'So, very well done!' Mr Carey (English, who never praises anyone), said: 'A first rate result…excellent. I am proud of you, young woman! On to the next stretch now!' (What does he mean by that?) Mademoiselle was pretty pleased as well. 'You 'ave done eet! I told you, work 'ard, and – voila! You 'ave zee result! *Formidable*!'

The headmaster has asked to see me – it can't be bad behaviour this time, can it? On my way up to his office, I nearly get knocked over by Jimmy Grant playing his

French horn and clicking his boots as a sort of syncopated accompaniment on each stone step as he runs down the stairs to the boys' changing rooms. (How can he possibly play and run at the same time? The horn is such a difficult instrument just standing still…) He has got a place at Cambridge to do music, apparently, and can't stop celebrating.

It turns out that the headmaster wants to ask me if, rather than leaving school this term, I wouldn't rather stay on and work at Latin in order to matriculate. Then I could try for entrance to Oxford to do English. It would mean special 'crash' coaching for a couple of terms, maybe a year – you have to have Latin or maths for Oxford entrance – but that could be arranged.

'You would have to work hard, but given your results I have no doubt you could do it'.

'I don't think my mother can afford it.'

'There are bursaries…'

'But I am going to art school,' I say, thinking Ma would be disappointed because Father was an artist and she wants me to be one, and anyway I have got a place at the Central School of Arts and Crafts starting next term.

'I'll write to your mother. We think English is the future for you.'

Does that mean they don't think art is the future? And what's so great about English? I like reading, and writing, but I don't want to spend my time only doing that, so why take an exam in it? I have had enough of exams anyway – I just want to draw. Besides, Peggy is going to the Central School next term to do theatre design, and I want to go with her.

I don't say any of this. Ma will soon put the headmaster straight.

I was in the history room today, and found Jane reading a report about Bomber Harris and his bombing campaign over Berlin. Jane was worrying about a German family she had stayed with in Berlin when she was a student. She seemed quite upset, but I hope they bomb them to pieces.

Bob and the school orchestra are rehearsing the Schumann piano concerto in the hall this afternoon (funny to think he was a German!) They are going to perform it at the end of term concert. He asked me if I would like to be his page turner, but very politely I said no thanks; he always gets so furious with everybody, including his page turners. There is a section at the end of the third movement where the rhythm suddenly goes completely wild, berserk, piano against orchestra, etc. Every time I hear it, my heart almost stops, so I would probably lose the place anyway.

This afternoon I go and listen to them rehearsing. Barbara is leading the orchestra, Vic playing the oboe, Jimmy French horn, Gervase clarinet and then the fiddle players augmented by various staff scratching away. They are practising the bit in the last movement where the beat gets so complicated and thrilling. The piano builds up and up to a great wave of sound, pauses, and then seems to topple over itself and cascade down in a wonderful tempestuous avalanche. It is a difficult piece time wise for the orchestra apparently, so they play this section several times, Bob getting increasingly sarcastic and ratty. But I never tire of hearing it, and sit listening as he makes them repeat it again and again.

The headmaster's remarks about staying on at school go niggling through my mind. *Would* I like to stay on at school for another year, two years, work and work at Latin, and finally go to Oxford? What does reading English mean? Anyway, where is Oxford? I'd rather be in London at art school with Peggy. (By the way, Peggy has changed her name to Karin! She says she has never felt like a Peggy, and Karin is her second name after her Russian grandmother or somebody.)

Peter is staying on here to do matric. Barbara is going to study for her first MB and then medicine. Only Peggy and I are leaving at Christmas from Form Two. In January I am going to be seventeen, and Ma says somehow or other we'll have a party – but I worry about it. Who would come? I wonder if I could ask Johan? He is leaving school this term, living out in Hendon somewhere and going to the London School of Economics.

Gervase lives in Hampstead, and I have just discovered that Simon Chan – who is going to Imperial College to do engineering, would you believe; I have quite gone off him – will be in Golders Green next year with his family! So, with Peggy, I mean Karin, that's four! I am looking forward to this party already.

IV
1944–1946
An End and a Beginning

I am not sure what I expected from art school, but it is not this! I wanted to go to the Central School of Arts and Crafts with Peggy, but there was a problem, and I've ended up in this dump (St Martin's), in Charing Cross Road. I don't know what I am supposed to be doing half the time, and the students are all much older than me and not particularly friendly.

One of them, Lucian Somebody, came into the life room today with a few of his snooty friends, laughing and joking and brandishing a violin. (He frightens me with his slanting eyes and thin smile.) He arranges the violin on a table with a piece of blue cloth and a couple of bottles, and then starts to draw watched by the others. After twenty minutes or so, he gets up and walks out, taking the violin and his admiring 'court' with him, but leaving the drawing behind. When I have a look I am astonished. In no time at all and with apparently no effort, he has created the most vivid and lifelike collection of objects which leap up off the page more real than the things themselves. I have never seen anyone draw like this, not even my father.

Life drawing is a forest of easels in a big shabby room, a crowd of loafing students all smoking and this poor old sagging woman sitting hour after hour for us to draw. I've never seen a fat old person's naked body before, but I would hide myself away if I looked like that, not take off all my clothes and stand in a room for forty students to stare at. Every now and then, the teacher comes round and hovers behind each person to look at their drawing. Sometimes he mumbles something, sometimes not. So far he has said nothing at all to me. The other class I am supposed to take part in is drawing from the antique – dusty cracked plaster casts of assorted hands and feet, heads of Roman senators, etc. Boring, boring – I don't want to stay here.

'That's fortunate,' Ma says when I tell her this. 'Because the bursar at the Central phoned today. Someone has dropped out and there is a place for you after all!'

Unfortunately, the Central is not much better. It is so big and dark and, like St Martin's, everybody seems to know where they are going and what they are doing except me. Peggy, known as Karin these days, is well into her theatre design course, so I don't see much of her. Ma says I should go on a course like her, get some sort of qualification. But what? After another long dreary morning of drawing from the antique, I am beginning to wish I had stayed on at school to do Latin.

On the news today we are told that 2,300 tons of bombs were dropped on Berlin last night. All our planes returned. What would happen if Simon and I were to be called up? I suppose he would go into the RAF and I would join the navy. Perhaps I should do that, instead of going to art school. Would I be on a boat – I mean, ship? Or would it just be sweeping the floor, or secretarial work?

As there is not enough room in the Belsize Park flat, my birthday party (rather late – I was seventeen at the end of January) is to be held in the house of a colleague of Ma's near Baker Street. Karin and one or two other students from the Central are coming (not many), and I have a new dress

– made by Miss Daisy, Margaret's little dressmaker lady in Kilburn. Lovely black taffeta with flowers embroidered on it left over from a film she worked on before the war. Off the shoulders, long, and crackling and rustling as I move.

There is music and Ma's colleague has invited a few Canadian airmen she knows stationed in London to build up the numbers of men as my friends are mostly girls! Good-looking and relaxed in their dress uniforms, they swoop into the room joking and chatting to everyone. They are excellent dancers, and it all goes with a terrific swing. I dance with one of the Canadians a lot – Fitch McKinnon. Funny name but quite nice. Before the end of the party he says wouldn't I like to meet again, what is my phone number? So I give it to him. We arrange to go to a film next week.

The film is on somewhere in the King's Road, and today I went to meet Fitch at a flat he shares with some other Canadian airmen in Markham Square, Chelsea.

It is a house not a flat, and has a creeper growing round the door which twists all over the front of the house up towards the balcony. I ring the bell, and for some reason I am quite nervous. Nice as he is, I don't know this Fitch very well (and I haven't told Ma about meeting him, as she always wants to know exactly where I am going, who with and what time I'll be back as if I am a child). Anyway, he opens the door and my heart sinks. He looks different, somehow older than I remember, smelling of beer, his face rather red and blotchy, and suddenly I wonder if I should have come, alone. We go into a big untidy room downstairs; he shares this house with four other airmen, apparently, their clothes and possessions everywhere and it stinks of sweat and cigarette smoke. He offers me a drink. I say tea, please…cigarette? I don't smoke, thanks – and we talk about the party. At first it's all right. He calls me a cool dame and laughs a lot, asks me about art school and what I am doing there – am I painting a lot of 'noodes'; he is 'damn well sure I look better "noode" than any model', etc. I say I am not painting anything, I am drawing, and there is a bit of a silence. I wish I hadn't come.

'This is a nice house,' I say, for something to say.

'The landlord is an artist guy. There's a studio upstairs, paintings. Yeah,' he says, smiling. 'Wanna have a look? Be my guest, kid…I'll give you a tour – as you're an expert.'

The room upstairs – a bedroom, by the way, not a studio – does have a few canvases stacked against the walls, and I am looking at one of them when Fitch suddenly comes up very close behind and grips me in a sort of bear hug (he's incredibly strong), and starts to push me towards the bed.

'Aw, come on, honey, don't give me a hard time,' he says, as I kick out at him and wriggle free. He is smiling.

'Little bitch,' he mutters softly. We stare at each other and he sort of grabs at me and then the front door downstairs bangs and someone is yelling, 'Fitch? *Fitch*? Message for you. Where are you? *F-I-T-C-H?*'

He goes to the door, calls down then leaves the room. I decide I am leaving too, but when I try to open the door it is locked. The window is open and, very quickly, I get out on to the balcony, swing my legs over and, holding the drainpipe, half climb, half fall, down the creeper. When I get to the bottom I run as fast as I possibly can out of the square into the King's Road, keep going until I reach Sloane Square, then slow down and look back. Nobody. Puffing like a steam engine, I jump on a nineteen bus before realising that I have left my bag – money and keys –

behind. So, have to get off and walk home. Julyan is sitting in the little library at the end of the road, homework still in his satchel, reading a *Beano* annual, so I use his key to get in. I don't tell Ma about anything. Just that I have lost my keys…and money. She is very cross – particularly about the keys – but I still don't tell her what happened.

Frankfurt was 'heavily' bombed last night with the loss of six of our aircraft. Mrs Jackson's husband (she lives in the flat below us) is in Bomber Command. I hope he wasn't in one of them.

Bomber Command is bombing Germany every night. A bit of me is sorry for them, but mostly I am glad. Mrs Jackson's husband is still all right. It's the rear gunners that get killed most, Simon says. They last about a fortnight.

I am now a student at the art department of Willesden Technical College! The plan is to do the National Diploma in Design, a three-year course ending in a further year at the Institute of Education. The first part, drawing, perspective, composition, design and lettering, will be at Willesden (I have missed a couple of terms and have to work harder than I ever have before, to catch up). The second part is at the Chelsea School of Art starting in the autumn of 1945 – painting, illustration, history of art and a craft. Then a year at the Ministry of Education learning how to teach. I don't particularly like Willesden, but at least they try and teach us something. I'll get the first part of the course over as quickly as I can, and move on to Chelsea for the more interesting second half – if all goes according to plan.

The Willesden students are completely different from the St Martin's and Central crowd. Younger, spotty, gawky, completely uninterested in 'Fine Art' – i.e. painting. Most of them want to be technical draughtsmen, cartoonists or go into commercial studios to do advertising stuff. They think I am 'stuck up' because I am not interested in that sort of thing, and because of the way I speak. (I don't particularly like the way they speak, but I don't say so.) I have one friend, Nina. She is interested in painting like me, and wants to go to Chelsea too. She also seems to be entirely crazy about horses – riding them, I mean. Odd.

An appointment in Hampstead with the dentist on 6th June – the same one I have been to ever since we were at Holly Place.

I didn't sleep well last night, so I am late getting up and eat my breakfast in a hurry. As soon as I am out in the street, it is obvious that something extraordinary is happening. For one thing the noise! A continuous and all pervading loud roar of engines. Aeroplanes. The whole sky – not just a small area, but right across from one side to the other – is filled with planes all flying in one direction, sun gleaming on the grey metal. As I walk up to Haverstock Hill, people are stopping on the pavement pointing up at the sky, laughing and talking about what it means.

The moment I get in to his consulting room, Mr Messenger, normally a quiet boring man, shouts: 'It's begun! The Second Front. At last! Started at six-thirty this morning! Have you seen the planes?' He is almost dancing about, jumping for joy!

Immediately I get home, I turn on the wireless.

With massive air support, waves of allied troops are landing on the beaches of Normandy. The operation began at six-thirty this morning, and heavy fighting is reported. The Allied Supreme Commander, General Eisenhower, is confident that bridgeheads are being established, and rapid progress is being made. He asks that our thoughts and prayers are with our brave soldiers in their endeavour. The prime minister Mr Churchill will speak to the nation at nine o'clock this evening. Bulletins on the progress of the fighting will be issued every hour.

When Ma is back from work, we keep the wireless on continuously, bulletin after bulletin.

After D-Day, there is a sort of subdued background 'atmosphere' to daily events. A mixture of excitement and dread, curiosity, pride. Everyone knows that this is 'it', a life and death struggle, not only for all the soldiers and airmen taking part but for saving the whole world from Hitler and his 'Naaarzis', as Mr Churchill calls them.

Today, I and one or two others from Willesden go to Studio One at Oxford Circus to see some Pathé news, and we watch the 'landings' film round twice. The noise is incredible, deafening. The roar and whine of aircraft, destroyers in the background firing their big guns, shells exploding, and the poor brave men in their tin hats wallowing up and down in the landing craft, then somehow jumping overboard into the water and wading ashore, rifles above their heads! How do they do it? The Germans have mined the shallow water, of course, so some of the landing craft are blown up before they get anywhere near. (We aren't shown this.) And the soldiers are so heavily weighed down with ammunition and the rest of their kit that if they stumble and fall in the water, or are wounded, it must be impossible for them to get up again. The destroyers shelling the German positions have barrage balloons protecting them, but the landing craft are horribly exposed. And once they are on the beach they have got the Germans ahead, machine gunning and blowing them to pieces.

On the news at breakfast the announcer says that 'Allied troops are consolidating after airborne landings'. It seems that the night before D-Day, aeroplanes pulled gliders full of soldiers inland over Normandy in the dark, to parachute down and rendezvous with attackers from the beach in the morning. (How do they know where to meet?) Churchill says: 'These landings took place with extremely little loss and with great accuracy…a very great degree of risk had to be taken in respect of the weather…the airborne troops are well established…fighting is in progress at various points.' ('Fighting in progress' probably means the most horrible face-to-face flame thrower and bayonets struggle one can possibly imagine.)

At breakfast the next day, there is a report on the news that the Germans are talking about a 'secret weapon' to be let loose on Britain as a revenge for the invasion.

'Propaganda,' Ma says as she gets her things together for the office. 'Don't take any notice. And Marjorie-Ann, I may have to be a bit late tonight, so could you please get back in good time? You could collect Julyan from the library, if you would, and give him some tea? He has a music lesson tomorrow, so he ought to practise.'

I am a bit fed up with this sort of thing, as it's always me who has to stand in for Ma, and Julyan is a law unto himself. When he gets home from school and if Ma is not back, he is supposed to wait for her, or me, while doing his homework in the little library at the end of the road. Or, let himself into the flat and practise his music. The trouble is, he often has other ideas about how to spend this time. For instance, recently he told me that sometimes he goes on a 'fishing' expedition in the Tube on the way back from school, which can make him late. He stands near the lift in Hampstead station looking pathetic, and pretends to have lost his fare money and can't get home. (He can even manufacture tears he told me!)

'Oh dear, I've lost my money…I don't know what to do!' Sob, sob… 'Can you possibly lend me sixpence for my ticket? My mummy will pay you back…' Etc., etc.

He comes home laughing and jingling the profits in his pocket. If Ma finds out, she gets furious and confiscates it, but she doesn't always know. One afternoon at half-term she gave him the money to go and see a film, and he didn't reappear until five hours later and Ma was on the point of ringing the police. He enjoyed the film so much he had seen it round twice!

He is not in the library and doesn't appear until long after Ma gets home, so she is cross – with me! Which is unfair. She gets so worried when he disappears – I don't know why; he always turns up in the end. Today, he took it into his head to take the Tube to Edgware at the end of the Northern Line to see what it looked like. Boring, apparently! Ma sat and made him practise for three quarters of an hour after tea, and I must say, although I don't exactly enjoy it, when he stops arguing with Ma and gets down to it, he really is improving.

The news at the moment is: Heavy fighting is taking place as our troops gradually move inland. Bomber Command continues to pound German defence lines. Mrs Jackson's husband is still alive.

I am fed up. I have been wearing the same dreary things day in day out and haven't had anything new for months – since last winter in fact – *and* there are holes in the only pair of shoes I want to wear. Sometimes I long for something NEW so much it feels like a pain – but, no money and no coupons. I am going to steal something, anything, soon, even if it does make me a thief! When I tell Ma this, she says she has a suggestion. She has still got one of Great Aunt Nellie's tablecloths made of the finest Irish linen packed away in a trunk under her bed. 'What about making a summer dress out of it? Linen is one of the best materials you can buy,' she adds, seeing the expression on my face. I am a bit dubious about the tablecloth aspect, but last year Ma had a blouse made out of parachute silk, no coupons, and it looked lovely.

'We could ask Miss Daisy to make it?'

The tablecloth is in a trunk full of Great Aunt Nellie's linen and old clothes, scraps of patchwork and fabric put there for safe keeping when she died. A musty damp paper smell wafts out of the trunk when Ma opens it.

'It smells of her!' I say.

'We'll wash it. You see, it will be lovely.'

'What's this?' I pull out a beautiful broad-ribbed cream velvet jacket, silk lined in blue and carefully packed in crackling layers of tissue paper.

'I don't know. A bed jacket, I think? You can't wear that in summer.'

'Yes I can. Over the linen dress!'

I saw Mrs Jackson in the street today, red-eyed and sniffling into her handkerchief, so I suppose it's happened at last:

her husband has been killed. But I discover later that it's only the cat that got run over.

When I get back from Willesden, Ma says that there has been a big air raid in South London, a barracks, with a lot of people dead! Oh bloody hell and damnation! I thought all that was finished?

Next day, everyone is talking about this latest air raid. It was carried out by Germany's new secret weapon, the V-1, a new sort of flying bomb. Pilotless. Two days later I see one over Holborn. It looks like a small plane in trouble, fire belching out of the tail and making a sound like a motor bike trying to get up a steep hill. Eventually, the engine cuts out and it dives to earth and explodes, blowing up whatever it lands on. The nickname, doodlebug, doesn't give any idea of how frightening and horrible it is.

One of them puttered over us this afternoon, dropped down somewhere in West Hampstead and exploded with a terrible bang. We get them every day now, and people are going down to the Tube again at night for shelter. At Belsize Park in the evening, the platforms are filled with people sleeping or trying to. Whole families, mothers, babies, grannies, everyone down there. But me and Ma and Julyan (Simon is at school) have decided to stay at home. We put mattresses along the inner wall of the passage in our flat, just next to the central well of the stone mansion stairs outside. This is because when places get knocked down, often the stairs remain standing. Usually I sleep, but sometimes it is impossible. First the air raid siren wails into action, then the guns get going, and after a while this grumbling muttering, sort of getting-slowly-nearer droning in the distance starts, which, as you listen, cuts out suddenly. That's the worst bit: waiting until you hear the explosion – sometimes quite far away, sometimes near. If it is near, you hear the rumble of masonry as the building collapses (other people being squashed to death this time). V-2s are being launched as well – rockets which blast everything flat for miles when they land. Also landmines on parachutes. You don't hear these last two coming.

I was lying on my mattress in the passage last night (the siren had gone), when I heard a funny fizzing creaking sound on the other side of the wall. I opened the front door and saw a river of flames pouring down the stone steps outside, so I shut the door quickly, stepped over the sleeping Julyan and went and told Ma – she was still up, doing the ironing. She took a little time to unplug the iron and put it somewhere safe, and when she opened the door the flames had died back a bit, leaving thick black smoke and an awful burning paint smell. It turned out that a couple of incendiaries had dropped through the skylight at the top of the stairs and flaming phosphorus, or whatever it is, had poured down the stone steps, through the main door which had been propped open for some reason, and out into the street. Each group of flats in the mansions has a bucket of water and a stirrup pump, and the ARP fire watcher man who came said you are meant to put out any incendiaries with that!

Last night there was a really bad raid – there must have been an absolute armada of them over London. The anti-aircraft guns banged away hour after hour and kept us awake, so in the end both Julyan and I got into Ma's bed with her and snuggled up together.

'Are you frightened?' I asked her.

'Certainly not!' she said, but I could feel her shaking.

I travel to college overland on the tube from Finchley Road. At one point the line is mounted on an embankment and there is a panoramic view across acres of railway track and

143

sidings, streets of little houses laid out like a fish's backbone, churches, clock towers, factories. Every morning there are new holes in this landscape.

Today, a house right up against the line between Neasden and Dollis Hill that I had often noticed from the train has vanished. Yesterday it had washing fluttering on a line from a first floor window, and a little flat roof where a baby in a sort of basket thing was put out in fine weather. This morning there is just a space, nothing underneath but a pile of rubble, that awful white dust still hanging in the air and a few ARP men in tin hats digging.

Art school is closed because of the summer holidays, and Nina, my horsey friend from Willesden, has asked me to go with her to Yorkshire and ride up on the moors there. She used to go to a co-ed school in one of the more remote valleys, Swaledale; and because her mother was ill a lot at the time she was a child, she often spent part of the holidays with a farming family there: one of the sons was a pupil at the school, and they are still very much in touch. Apparently they are going to let us live in one of their farm cottages for a week or so, and lend us a couple of ponies as well. I haven't ridden a horse since my first boarding school!

Mr and Mrs Houghton have such pronounced Yorkshire accents I find it hard to understand them. The son is easier. It is a large farm, hundreds of acres extending down and across the plunging dale and up to the moors above, dry stone walls following and defining the contours of the land. Having known the family since she was eleven, and with access to miles of wild and beautiful country often on horseback, it is all like a second home to Nina.

144

The grey stone cottage is dark and primitive: no kitchen, no bathroom, just an Elsan in a shed on the far side of the little yard, cold slate floors, camp beds, a primus stove, and a pump at the back door. We dump our sleeping bags, bring in some logs to make a fire later, and walk up to the farm to collect milk and some eggs for supper. Tomorrow the ponies.

'Let them find their way,' Nina calls the next day, after we have saddled up and are ambling slowly along the stony track to higher ground. 'They know what they are doing much better than us.'

As we get higher, a huge sweeping landscape begins to open out. Miles and miles of uneven rough ground, heather and bracken with grassy sheep trails between, along which now the ponies begin to trot.

'Keep away from the green patches,' Nina yells against the wind. 'They're bogs…once you fall in one of those, you're a goner!'

In the valley, flies and midges torment us and the ponies, but not up here. Cantering across the grassy uplands a cool breeze blows in our faces and we are insect free. We ride for an hour or so across a succession of high ridges, scree and bracken plunging away on either side until we reach another sheep-dotted wild dale sloping steeply into a dark valley. Hot and sweaty, we follow the stream trickling down towards a clump of rowan trees and birch, tether the ponies and find a waterfall cascading into a cleft between the rocks and a pool deep enough to swim in. The water is black and so cold it almost cuts you in half; but we splash around, jump and dive off one of the rocks, and then sit in the hot sun wolfing down our bread and cheese.

On Saturday night we go up to the farm to have baths, and Mrs Houghton asks us if we would like to come to

Sunday dinner – 'as a change from beans on toast'! So at one o'clock the next day, we are welcomed into the big farm kitchen where Mrs Houghton – a spreading red-faced woman, she has had eleven children! – is dishing up roast lamb. Mr Houghton, Arthur – the son still at home – the two married daughters and four grandchildren, plus the Italian prisoner of war farm worker are all sitting round the massive kitchen table, laughing and talking and I can't understand a word. Mrs Houghton calls the Italian 'the eye-tie', and he speaks very broken English made worse by a completely incomprehensible Yorkshire accent!

We have leg of lamb roasted and crisp from the oven, mint sauce and gravy, roast potatoes, cabbage, braised onions and carrots, apple pie and baked custard, and strong dark tea to finish. You would never think there was a war going on, or things called ration books. I have never seen so much food all together on a table in my whole life. I suppose it's because it's a farm. In fact Mr Houghton tells me that we are eating one of his late lambs, and Mrs Houghton and the 'eye-tie' grow all their own vegetables. Nina and I eat until we are full to bursting, and then sit in front of the range with its two kettles hissing and steaming, listening to Mr Houghton talk about the farm, his sheep, and what the war means for farmers. (It's good, apparently, but will be bad again as soon as the war is over.) They give us home-cured bacon to take back with us for breakfast, as well as eggs. No shortage of those either, as they have their own hens. It is another world – and suddenly I think of our little kitchen in the flat at Belsize Park, and start worrying. Have there been more raids? Are they all right? In the evening we walk the two miles down to the valley road where there is a telephone box.

'Raids?' Ma says. 'What raids? Everything is fine.'

A friend of Ma's living at Steeles's Studios round the corner, Peter Kapp, is having a party and has invited me – I don't know why. A little round man, a painter with stand-up black curly hair, he knew Picasso in Paris – he says! Is he a bit of a boaster? He also says he wants to paint my portrait.

I like his studio better than his paintings, which are highly coloured and rather crude, lots of paint slapped on with a palette knife. The studio is full of people, including an American GI called Curt Stransky in an immaculate uniform who comes over to talk to me. After the Fitch experience, I am a bit suspicious, but he is quiet and gentle and asks me if I live with my family and where. So I say yes, my mother and two brothers, about two minutes' walk away. He says how much he misses his mother and father (he has been away in the army now for nearly two years). So as it's only round the corner, I ask him if he would like to meet my mother and family, and he seems very pleased. Before that, our painter host claps his hands asking for silence, and says that the point of the party is to celebrate the genius of a young friend of his, Norman or Norbert Somebody, a violinist, who works in a factory in Camden Town and before that was on the Isle of Man in a detention centre for enemy aliens. The moment he begins to play, the room becomes completely hushed and quiet. I have never heard a violin sound like this before, like velvet, or dark, rich, musical chocolate. He is quite young, with black hair growing very low on his forehead, and thick black horn-rimmed glasses. He plays and plays – Bach, I think – and every time it seems as if he is going to stop, the other guests clap and call out, persuading him to continue. At last, our host raises his glass and says, 'Thank you, my friend. It has been a privilege to hear you. Magnificent! Here's to your great career!' And we all drink a toast. After that I say I must go, as I have promised to be back by eleven-thirty. Curt offers to walk me round to the flat.

'What floor are you on? Do your family have a shelter?' he asks.

'Yes, but we don't use it.'

'You should,' he says very seriously.

Ma likes him very much. Asks him to come and visit when he can.

'I would be glad to, ma'am,' he says.

I wish Ma would wear nicer clothes. She embarrasses me; she looks such a frump most of the time – old, with lines on her forehead, and wrinkles. When she has had her hair done and puts on some make-up, doesn't have to go to work and is laughing about something, she can be quite pretty. But it doesn't last. She remembers something she has to do, and starts looking old and worried again.

Sometimes I help her with the ironing, or take the washing to the laundrette, but those sorts of things are quite boring. Today I clean the flat, but the boys mess it up again almost at once; just leave their stuff around, and make it as bad as it was before I cleaned it. Ma says that perhaps when the war is over, we could move back to Hampstead and have a house and garden of our own. Meantime the horrible V-1s and 2s go on and on, and so does the war. Allied troops are in Florence, the Russians getting near Warsaw, the brave Poles battling their way out to meet them. In the Pacific the Americans are fighting a war with the Japanese.

In the Underground today, there was a family who looked as if they had walked straight out of some sort of incident – flying bomb or worse – their clothes dishevelled and dusted over with bits of plaster and grit; a father, a mother and four quite young children, about seven, six, five, and four, each one very much like the other. I don't think they were English – although they didn't say anything, didn't speak at all either in English or anything else. They got in at Charing Cross, and sat opposite me, six pairs of dark eyes staring at me as if they had seen something terrible, which they probably had. I smiled at the children once or twice, but none of them smiled back. They looked as if they would never smile again.

So that we can have a break from the doodlebugs, we are having a week in someone's house in Welwyn Garden City. And today Simon and I watched another dogfight going on high up above the cornfields, but this time nobody got shot down. Disappointing for Simon.

Ma is upset because since August the Poles have been trying to fight their way out of Warsaw and the Russians are just sitting there not helping them. They hate the Poles, apparently, so they don't mind the Germans killing them all. Curt Stransky, whose grandfather was Polish, is coming for the day to visit us on Sunday. Last time I saw him, he told me about the Russian/Pole thing, and also that American forces have handed Paris back to the Free French.

Curt is taking me dancing! It is his birthday, so I gave him a handkerchief (one coupon), with a 'C' embroidered by me in the corner. He is much older than me – twenty-three.

We go to a club crammed with soldiers, airmen, sailors, all of different nationalities: Free French, New Zealanders, Canadians. Their girls are smoking and very made-up and glamorous. I feel embarrassed, as I am convinced they all know my dress is made out of a tablecloth! Curt says I look better than all of them put together, but I don't really believe him. Some Polish airmen are sitting together in a huddle looking really miserable and angry. Because of trying to fight their way out of Warsaw and nobody helping them, I suppose.

I have told Ma that I am perfectly alright on my own, but she has made Curt promise to bring me home himself, so just after eleven we get hold of a grumpy taxi driver. He mutters something about how he was just going home and anyway there are too many bloody Yanks around, but in the end he takes us. Somewhere near Camden Town he drives into a street which, halfway along, has been taped off to prevent access.

'Unexploded bomb,' one of the fire watchers shouts. 'Take the detour.' But the taxi driver refuses to go any further – he has to get home, he says – so we walk the rest of the way. I asked Curt if he would like to spend Christmas with us, but he said he may not be in London much longer, because the Americans have captured Manilla, capital of the Philippines, and he may be going in that direction. (Where are the Philippines?)

We have been invited to the Boswells's for Christmas. Ma is going to take a Christmas pudding – mostly carrot and swede, breadcrumbs, rendered fat and a very few currants, I expect – plus our ration books. She hasn't got any dark brown sugar or molasses, so she says she is going to colour the pudding with tea or perhaps gravy browning! Jean Boswell, Ma's friend, is a portrait painter, and Mr

Boswell works in the BBC and is a member of the British Communist party (like Luli Reif). He thinks that Britain should have the same sort of government as the Soviet Union, and he and Ma argue about it. They go at it like quarrelling children, louder and louder and quite cross. So I don't know what Christmas will be like.

The two older Boswell boys went to my school, although I didn't really know them there. One is doing medicine, and the other wants to be a farmer. At school he wore steel-tipped army boots and went rattling about the place in corduroy trousers tied up with baling twine, mole traps and rabbit gins jingling from a brass-studded leather belt he always wore. People said he kept an airgun in his dormitory, but I don't know if that was true. I have a feeling he didn't go to many lessons. The older brother is exempted from war service because he is at a hospital studying to be a doctor, but the younger one has been called up. He is a conscientious objector though, which means he has to work on a farm instead – which is what he wanted to do in the first place! Clever, really.

1945

I had a letter from Curt today. He says: 'Hello Sunshine, I have an office in New York. One day you must visit me here...' He writes nice letters, but I don't really miss him too much as I have met up with David, who is studying to be a doctor and lives in Hampstead almost next door to Gervase. He used to be at my school, but older, and I don't remember him. He plays the fiddle and still has lessons – and sometimes he and Gervase get together and play chamber music. Last week I spent an evening at David's home, in company with a lot of musician friends of his including the violinist I first heard at Peter Kapp's party. There he was, horn-rimmed specs gleaming, playing Mozart with his newly formed quartet, The Amadeus. I never thought I would meet him again but he and David have the same violin teacher, who sometimes comes to play with them. I think I ought to bring Julyan to listen, it sounds so wonderful and extraordinary. Beautiful. I want it to go on forever.

Apart from Kenwood when I was a child, I have never been in a house (which is a home) as big as David's – an imposing red-brick mansion, with well-proportioned spacious rooms, dark old furniture and lots of paintings. In the room where they have music, there is a Picasso above the sideboard, signed. A rather stylised nude woman kneeling on a beach. A lot of greenish blue. Quite nice.

The RAF are bombing Berlin and other German cities every night – we get told which ones the next day. Last night it was Dortmund, Essen, Ems, Hamburg, Berlin and probably some others I have forgotten. The Americans have begun crossing the Rhine over the Remagen Bridge and General Eisenhower has called on Germany to surrender. (They haven't yet.) Montgomery and the British Army are on German soil, and the Russians are fifty miles from Berlin. Ma says they are all racing each other to get there first. She thinks that with luck the war could be over this summer. I hope she's right.

Meanwhile the V-1s and 2s are worse than ever, and the doodlebug raids have got so bad we decide to try sleeping down in the Underground. Big mistake. For some reason Maggie's little dog Boppo is staying with us at the moment, so he had to come too. A little King Charles the First or

Second spaniel thing, very stupid. Anyway, when the siren goes, we get everything together, brush our teeth and have a last wee – no toilets down there – and walk up to Belsize Park, the second deepest Underground station in London

Of course we haven't done it before, so we don't have a 'place'. People have their own regular bunks or little bits of the platform where they go every evening – like having a family pew in church, if one is the sort of family that goes to church, which we are not.

It is cheerful and warm down there, with bunk beds and trains coming and going; but noisy – people coughing and smoking, talking, babies crying. As soon as we find some space, a cross-looking lady wrapped in a red blanket sits up and starts on at Ma about Boppo.

'Is that your dog?'

'My stepdaughter's–'

'Dogs ain't allowed down here.'

'Well, we can't leave him behind! He barks and keeps people awake!' (I had to laugh at this, because really it's the bombs and gunfire that are keeping people awake – if they are not killed first, of course.) 'He's no trouble,' Ma says, and immediately, Boppo begins to growl and then bark like a maniac at an imaginary dog guarding someone's sleeping bag two bunks away.

'Bloody dogs!' the woman says, pulling the blanket back over her head.

A train comes clattering in and somebody starts shouting about something down at the far end of the platform, but there are no doodlebugs or ack-ack guns, which is a relief. We lie on our mattresses and Julyan chatters away to the red blanket lady, who seems to have forgotten about Boppo. Simon reads his book, and I try to sleep. After a while I hear the sound of water rushing, and see the man next door peeing gallons into a bottle balanced between his legs.

'Niagara Falls,' Simon says, and we start laughing and can't stop. The man complains to Ma, and says we are noisy kids out of control keeping him awake; when he was young, children knew how to behave, etc., etc. In the end none of us sleeps much, so after that we decide to stay at home.

Maggie phoned to say that she has been sent some wool cloth from the USA which she doesn't need – would I like it for a coat or something? She is tremendously busy with her ambulance work at the moment, so I have to collect it from her ambulance garage place between Finchley Road and St John's Wood stations at the end of her shift tonight. She does eight hours on, another eight hours standby, and then eight hours official 'time off' – unless there is an emergency, in which case she has to stay on duty. She says she's exhausted and actually she doesn't look too good. The dark navy uniform and ambulance driver's peak cap somehow accentuate her green-white face with its gash of lipstick and cigarette.

She is sitting smoking and drinking tea with a first-aid man and a couple of telephonists in a dark smoky little office in one corner of the lock-up garage. The next shift haven't turned up, which means that, willy-nilly, Maggie and the first-aid man will have to stay on and report for duty if the siren goes. The last few nights have been free of doodlebug raids, so we drink our tea and hope they'll leave us alone. No such luck. I am opening my parcel – lovely plum-coloured tweed – when the siren starts up, and very soon we hear the guns. The telephone starts to ring.

154

'Right, us next.' Maggie crushes out her cigarette and looks at me. 'You had better stay here until the all clear–' and she doesn't finish her sentence, as an almighty bang rattles the windows and almost knocks us off our seats. The familiar awful rumble of falling bricks and stone follows, and then another terrible bang.

One of the telephonists is talking into the phone.

'Painswick Street? Yes, King's Cross… We have one ambulance here, but we are short of first-aid personnel… Yes… A block of flats… Pentonville Road? OK.' She looks at Maggie. 'They've got some medics there already but need another ambulance?' Maggie and the first-aid man are already on their feet buckling on their gear.

'I'll come with you,' I say, not liking the idea of being left behind in the garage which, I notice suddenly, has a ceiling made up of mostly two very large glass skylights.

'No, you stay here!' They are halfway out of the door.

'But Belsize Park is–'

'Civilians are not allowed in ambulances!' snaps Maggie.

'I am your sister.'

'I will not be responsible–'

'But–'

'Let's get going,' the first-aid man interrupts.

'Maggie!'

'It's completely against the rules,' Maggie says as I follow them out. 'I'll drop you at Chalk Farm, end of discussion!'

I climb up behind them and she slams into gear. Very quickly we are out of the empty garage and whizzing along the Finchley Road towards Swiss Cottage. But then there is a 'diversion', and she becomes so preoccupied with the detours and damaged roads and being forced to take a long way round to get to King's Cross, she gives up about me. Now and then I say 'shall I get out here?' – to which she replies: 'Don't be an idiot!' And then, 'For God's sake make sure you are wearing a bloody tin hat!'

Peabody buildings look as if they have received a direct hit from something, maybe a landmine. Most of the centre of the block of flats has collapsed, and a pall of smoke and that choking white dust hangs over everything: I am already grinding grit between my teeth as the ambulance draws up. There must be whole families buried in there.

'You stay in the vehicle!' Maggie barks at me.

Firemen have their hoses trained on the fire leaping up on the far side of the building, and on top of the broken masonry and rubble, a policeman and some ARP personnel in tin hats are pulling out bricks and lumps of stone, throwing them to the side. A fireman comes over to us carrying a small child.

'God knows how many more are under all that,' he says, 'but this one's alive.'

Maggie bends over the child, a little girl.

'What's your name, darling?'

'She's OK…just shocked,' the fireman says.

We wipe her face, persuade her to sip some water, rinse the dirt and grit out of her mouth. Maggie tries to get her to say something, but she just stares at us, speechless.

'They are trying to free a woman with a smashed leg,' the man says, 'and we've got two others that need to get to hospital…hang on will you, until we can bring them over?'

Maggie and the fireman walk off to check the numbers, and I sit holding the child – who sags motionless against me, muttering: 'Mummy… Mummy…'

'She'll be here soon,' I say.

'Mummy… Mummy…'

'She's just coming…very soon. Shall I tell you a story while we wait? Once upon a time, there was a beautiful grey dolphin – a magic fish – swimming deep down in the green-blue sea…'

I keep rambling on until the first-aid men have got the stretcher cases into the ambulance, and Maggie has switched on the engine and we are bumping over potholes and lumps of concrete towards the Pentonville Road. One of the first-aid men (a medical student, he says) is administering oxygen, and I am still telling my story quietly, the little girl lying across my knees listening with her eyes half closed. After quite some time, the other medic, an older man, swivels round to look at us.

'How's she doing?' he says.

'Gone to sleep, I think.'

He holds the little wrist between thumb and forefinger for a moment, peels back an eyelid, puts a hand on her chest and then calls to the medical student to help him with the oxygen cylinder. He gets the mouthpiece in place, supporting the child's head on his knee. I watch all this, not understanding.

'No good,' he says at last. 'There's no pulse. No pulse at all. I'm sorry…nothing to be done. I am so sorry…' he says again, more emphatically. I suppose he thinks I am a relative. It is several minutes before I take in the fact that the child is dead. She died while I was telling her my stupid story.

I can't remember much about what happens next, except that when the all clear goes I am walking up the Hampstead Road to Belsize Park in my tin hat. As I let myself into the flat, Ma calls out: 'You are very late, have you had something to eat? I'm afraid the boys have finished the macaroni cheese…' I go into her bedroom and burst into tears. I thought she would be angry about going in

157

the ambulance, but she just hugged me and said she was glad I was safe.

That night I can't sleep. I keep thinking about the little girl and wondering whether the doctor in the ambulance could have saved her if he had attended to her first. When I talked to David about it the next day, he said that the child had probably died of shock combined with breathing in all those poisonous fumes and dust, and there was nothing that could have been done. But I keep thinking that if I hadn't been in the ambulance, she might have been seen more quickly by the doctor and not died.

At Chelsea I am to do drawing and painting from life, composition and still life, illustration, history of art and a craft – lithography in my case. Meanwhile I go plodding on at Willesden – exams due in the summer. Ron, a student in my year, says he is in love with me – will I marry him! Silly fool. He knows nothing about me, and vice versa.

More music at David's house. Their cook, a large broad-faced Dutch woman, won't allow people in her kitchen and chases us out when we go in to make a pot of tea, or search for some biscuits! On music evenings, however, when everyone is having a break and laughing and discussing what they have just played, she appears with a tray of cakes and sandwiches, a silver tea pot and hot water jug, cream in a little cut-glass jug.

David is Jewish, and he told me recently that in the course of their advance south across Germany the British have just discovered a truly nightmarish concentration camp. (It has been on the news, but I missed it.) Crowds of starving, dying people, mostly Jews but others as well, wandering aimlessly amongst literally thousands of corpses, other prisoners who had just died or, in some cases, been dead for days, even weeks. David assures me it is true – there are photos, which he has seen. I keep asking myself, what is it with the Germans? How can they? Why? The RAF are bombing Berlin twenty-four hours a day at the moment, and I am really glad.

Mr Roosevelt has died. Which is a pity as everyone believes that the war in Europe is coming to an end any minute, and after all his efforts he won't be there to see it. There has been heavy fighting round Berlin and the German armies are surrounded. It's extraordinary, you can feel this electric sort of jubilation in the air; strangers in the street smiling and asking each other for news.

At Willesden, too, everyone is talking about it – Hitler in his bunker with Eva Braun, and our troops, the Allies, entering Berlin. They are still meeting resistance from old men, a few boys of fifteen and younger who risk being hanged by the SS if they refuse to fight. But it won't be long now. Today or tomorrow, this week or next, Nazi Germany will be beaten and the war will be over.

I find it hard to believe.

At last! On the news this morning, we hear that the battle of Berlin has ended and the Germans have surrendered unconditionally. Hitler is dead, having committed suicide with Eva Braun in his bunker. Germany has a new leader, Admiral Doenitz (I don't envy him!), and the ceasefire takes effect at one minute past midnight tonight. Tomorrow is VE Day, when the Allied victory and the end of the war in Europe will be celebrated officially – although actually people have started already. The porter and some helpers were putting up bunting and flags when I got back to the flat from Willesden, and Ma said that in Westminster where she works people were milling around laughing and singing, and the buses were having trouble getting along Victoria Street and through Trafalgar Square, it was so crowded. One group of sailors had pulled down a row of wooden hoardings and were lighting bonfires, and the police just looked on smiling.

At eight, there is a knock on our door. It is Mrs Jackson from downstairs. Her daughter's baby arrived early this morning, and she wants to talk to Ma about it, and also did Ma think that the war is really over? Because that would mean that Squadron Leader Jackson, who is still alive, will be coming home, and the daughter in question doesn't have a husband. The father of the baby is an American serviceman who was killed somewhere in northern Germany in March, and she doesn't know what her husband will say. Extraordinary to think of ordinary things like babies being born just going on and on. Somehow I expect everything to stop in its tracks.

Today, 8th May 1945, World War Two has officially ended in Europe. A national holiday has been declared, and Ron and some of the other students at Willesden telephone to say that they are all going down to Trafalgar Square – will I come? I am not sure why, but I say no, I'd rather not (I am sure they think it's because I am 'stuck up'). Of course I am glad that the war – at least in Europe – is over, but I can't help feeling a sort of terrible heavy sadness. All those people who have died, the men and women who will never come back, death and destruction. The starving scarecrows of the concentration camp, for example, thousands of pilots and soldiers, sailors and merchant seamen killed, not to mention the civilians all over Europe, millions of them. And yet somehow we are alive. How? Why? (I know it's a question that no one can answer.)

Preparations for a party are well ahead down in the street. Trestle tables have been dragged out from somewhere, and bunting and flags festoon all the little balconies in front of the flats. Higgins is sitting at one of the tables drinking beer and wearing a Union Jack paper hat! Ma has taken Julyan to see the crowds in Trafalgar Square – 'The end of World War Two, something to remember,' she says. So I decide I'll stay in and do something energetic, constructive. Clean the flat from top to bottom and give her a surprise, maybe go to the street party later.

I start cleaning: the boys' room, Ma's bedroom, the hall, the kitchen, the front room. I even do the greasy old gas stove and last night's frying pan full of cutlery left to soak. When she gets back, leaving Julyan downstairs 'helping', I am finishing off the bathroom. Apparently, there are thousands and thousands of people out on the streets. Piccadilly and Trafalgar Square were already packed solid at midday; everyone happy and friendly, ecstatic that the war is finally over. She makes some tea, and gets out a packet of chocolate biscuits she has been hiding. We sit and talk about everything we can remember about what's been happening for the last six years. (She hasn't noticed that I have spring-cleaned the flat, and I wonder what the point of doing it is.) At three o'clock Mr Churchill speaks to the nation on the wireless, and the speech is relayed over loud speakers in Trafalgar Square. We sit and listen in our little kitchen (oilcloth on the table gleaming and clean, cutlery and crockery all put away, everything shipshape for once).

'…almost the whole world combined against the evil-doers who are now prostrate before us,' the familiar voice rolls out. 'We may allow ourselves a brief period of rejoicing; but let us not forget for a moment the toil and effort that lie ahead…' – he means Japan by this. 'We must now devote all our strength and resources to the completion of our task…' By the time he has got to the end, we are both in tears.

'I tell you what,' Ma wipes her eyes, 'we can start looking for a house!'

'With a garden?'

'Definitely.'

'When?'

'Very soon!'

'Will I have a bigger room?'

'Definitely!'

Part one of the drawing exam is over, and I am praying that I have got though it OK. Then I never will have to go to Willesden again, do another bloody perspective drawing or listen to Ron's drivel. I can hardly believe it, but recently he said to me that it's my fault that people fall in love with me (he means himself by this) – I shouldn't be so attractive! Wear sackcloth and ashes perhaps?

With the exception of Ron, boys are OK, but they are all sex maniacs – even David. And quite apart from Ma's lectures whenever I go out with anybody of the opposite sex, I don't fancy the idea of ending up with a dear little baby by mistake. As for being Mrs Somebody with kids and all that, no thanks! The sooner I get to Chelsea School of Art and start painting and drawing properly, the better.

Ron says I am abnormal. And if he was not so polite, David would probably say the same.

There is going to be an election, and everybody is getting very excited. Ma tries to explain the difference between Labour and Conservative to me. I may have misunderstood her, but how can anybody *ever* vote willingly for the Conservatives? Selfish rich people voting for themselves?

On Sunday, Uncle Toby comes with us to look at a possible house and give advice. His clothing coupon book has not come through yet, so he is still in uniform. There are dozens of empty houses and flats for sale are all over London, but we want to live in Hampstead because of the Heath, and because that's where we lived before the war.

The possible house is in Oak Hill Park, where Julyan's strange school used to be. Uncle Toby, who is supposed to know about 'property', says it's a bargain and a good time to buy. But when I see this rotting derelict old mansion, I wonder. It is gigantic, has an overgrown wilderness of a garden, a sort of subterranean netherworld of damp cellars and coal holes deep in a basement; three floors of bashed-about rooms, and an attic floor at the top 'lent' to a Polish refugee couple with a new baby and an Alsatian dog. (The three floors below them have dried-up pyramids of dog shit in every room.)

'Isn't it much too big, Toby?' Ma sounds worried.

'For the money, no. Just let out some of it,' he says. 'Pay for the mortgage.'

'What about the war damage?'

'It's not that bad…anyway, you will get a grant.'

'And the Polish couple?'

'Sitting tenants…that's why it is so cheap. But they'll leave sooner or later.'

It turns out that the war damage is rather more serious than Toby thought – a bad crack right through the centre of the house down into the foundations making it unstable. And although the government will pay for some repairs, it is still going to cost a lot. Too much, I am glad to say.

Toby says he has joined something called the Commonwealth Party and is thinking of voting for them in the election and so are a lot of ex-servicemen like him. Ma tells him that she is going to vote Labour and so should he, and they have an argument about it which lasts the whole of the time it takes to walk back to Belsize Park across the Heath.

It is embarrassing when Ma gets like this. Angry and red in the face, she argues more and more loudly, and people start to look at her in the street as if she is a maniac.

'Better to be wrong with charm than right without,' I remind her (she often says this to me). This makes her furious with me as well.

The results of the election have been announced and there has been a Labour landslide! Poor Mr Churchill! Saved us in the war and now nobody wants him. Ma is thrilled. Clement Attlee, who was only deputy prime minister in the last government, is the real thing now.

Everybody is talking about the 'New Britain', but I wonder if it will be as new as all that. For instance, I thought that the war finally being over would mean the end of clothing coupons and ration books. But the government says there will have to be more rationing not less!

There are long discussions going on everywhere about the governments's new free health service. This is because the minister for health, ex-miner Aneuran Bevan, has let it be known that he wants and intends to nationalise hospitals and doctors, and have a free health service for everyone – especially people who until now have been unable to afford it and so never got to a doctor – and there is a great fuss going on.

It seems a good idea to me, but some doctors are very much against it, and the British Medical Association is saying that Mr Bevan will destroy the doctor/patient relationship if his plans are put into action – I am not sure how. Dear old Dr Barton, our GP, has written to all his patients telling them that, should the new scheme actually become law, he is not going to take part in it. David says that most young doctors and medical students like him are all for it, and it is only the old guard who are against. Ma is always telling me how much she likes David, he is so kind and polite – considerate, unlike me! He will be a very good doctor, but I think he should be a musician he plays the violin so beautifully.

Simon and I are at Itchenor about to go off sailing in Ma's little dinghy, *Curlew*. Last night, we went to inspect the Pidcock's ancient green-and-white-painted barge, still moored here, and found it completely waterlogged. On a rising tide the water leaks through the cracks and warped planking until, still sitting on the mud, she is submerged. Then, as the ebbing tide recedes she slowly reappears, water pouring out of her. Poor old girl, she'll never float again.

It's a bright sunny day and we are walking down the main street towards the Hard, when suddenly, outside the village shop, we catch sight of what's written on the board outside. *Truman drops Atom bomb on Japan! Hiroshima! Thousands dead, thousands more wounded and missing!*

Sailing down towards Hayling Island, Simon tries to explain what 'splitting the atom' means and how you do it. But after a while he gives up because I don't get any of it, and anyway there is quite a lot of wind and I can't hear what he is saying. When we get home, Ma is still reading the paper. She looks shocked.

'Thirty per cent of the population dead...eighty thousand people, many more wounded or missing.' She shakes her head.

'At least the Germans didn't invent it first and try it out on us,' Simon says. Ma is in tears, and shakes her head again. Three days later, they drop another one on Nagasaki. On 15th August 1945, Japan surrenders. The Second World War, which has been going on since I was twelve, is over.

Today, in Studio One, I saw a film of the city of Berlin as the Allied bombers have left it. If an earthquake had struck it couldn't be worse, with survivors living in holes in the rubble. Impossible not to feel sorry for them, in spite of everything. I haven't seen any photographs or films of Hiroshima and Nagasaki yet, and I don't want to.

At last I have started at Chelsea! The principal is Harold Williamson, painter and commercial artist. (Did I hear that he is the man who put the 'O' in the Polo mint ad?) He gives the new students a pep talk on the first morning; what classes we will be doing, who is teaching what, when the first exams take place, where the canteen is, etc. Many of the staff, recently back from the war, are new themselves. Brian Robb, an illustrator, is still in uniform, and I think Edward Ardizzone is new too. He is teaching still life, which seems odd. Why not illustration? Harold Jones, another illustrator, is teaching lithography, and a brawny, serious man with a strong Yorkshire accent, Henry Moore, is in charge of the sculpture department. (I have seen some of his drawings of people asleep in the Underground at a Leicester gallery show.) Ceri Richards, a painter, is taking life drawing and painting, and there is Robert Medley, Sarah Nechamkin, Raymond Coxon, lots of them. Henry Moore is taking life classes too – for the sculpture students only, officially, but sometimes Nina and I manage to creep in; he is such a brilliant teacher.

Still life is the first class I do, taken by 'Call me Ted' Ardizzone. He is jolly and absent-minded, taking snuff every ten minutes or so and sneezing into a large red-spotted handkerchief; the front of his jersey is speckled with it. He looks exactly like a figure in one of his own drawings, and spends most of the session drawing the subject himself in a little square sketchbook – fruit in a bowl on a wood-topped table. During the last ten minutes, however, he wanders round the room talking and looking at our drawings while munching one of the still-life apples! In the afternoon, it is painting from the nude figure – in this case a regular stick-insect female.

The students at Chelsea are different from Willesden. Most of the men are ex-service so they have received grants from the government, and are older, more serious and more interesting. Gerry, for example, who has fought his way across Europe to Berlin, is half French and paints apples and plates on a checked tablecloth just like Bonnard; Nick, a tall devil-may-care ex-naval man who spent the war on minesweepers, already draws so beautifully it takes my breath away; and John, short-sighted and clumsy, bumps into easels or other people's paintings while forever expostulating about the meaning of Art, the purpose of

Art, Capitalist Art, Socialist Art, Art-Art-Art leaking out of him like water from a colander. Sometimes we have to shout at him to shut the hell up!

Nick is the one I like; I could get swept up by him. At first I thought it was the way he draws, but of course it's more than that.

Tonight there is a party at someone's flat in the King's Road, and Nick and some of the older students arrive with bottles of wine and we all talk a lot and dance – and drink. I don't like wine much, but it makes me feel happy and not care about anything. One of the girls got a bit too happy (drunk), started taking all her clothes off and was about to go out in the street completely naked, until two of us stopped her. I stayed on so late, I missed the last Tube. We went on drinking and talking until it began to get light, and I couldn't keep my eyes open any longer. The divan was occupied by variously drunk and amorous students and there was a clamour for me to join them. But I didn't fancy it somehow, all hugger-mugger like that. So I slept on some cushions on the floor with a rug over me. I am not sure where Nick got to. I woke up stiff and sore and with my head aching.

When I got back the next day, I had a blinder of a row with Ma about not telling her where I was, and not coming home. She said that I was being thoroughly selfish and inconsiderate, and that she had enough on her plate without worrying about me and whether I was under a bus. I said of course I wasn't under a bus, just having a good time. I was eighteen – grown-up – everybody stayed on at parties, and there was nothing to worry about. She said as long as I lived with her, she was responsible, which meant I must always phone her and let her know if I wasn't

168

coming home and where I was going to be. I said that was OK, but one couldn't always find a phone box or have the right change, and anyway parties sometimes blew up at the last minute, and what was wrong with dossing down in someone's flat like everyone else? I am not a child, I said. To which she replied, 'Don't behave like one then!' The argument spluttered on and on until we were both shouting and getting nowhere. My mother! She doesn't know the half of what goes on, and I'm certainly not telling her…

Life drawing and the stick insect again for a week or two, but today there is a model to make one sit up and really *look*! A tiny graceful figure about the size of a thirteen-year-old child, orange curls and violently made-up face, a delicate little thin body wreathed in diaphanous mauve and purple scarves, plus an assortment of bangles and chains clinking together like a harness. He – it is a man; no breasts, and a sequined pouch to hold his 'bits' together – looks as I have always imagined Ariel in *The Tempest* to be. A sprite, a fragile magical creature – half human, half fairy – ready to spring up into the air, disappear in a shower of stardust.

In fact, after a lot of stretching and posturing, all he does is settle into a pose which is so dramatic it is almost funny. He keeps the pose with hardly a tremor, but the moment the minute-hand reaches the hour he slips into a purple satin dressing gown, takes out a packet of gold-tipped Balkan Sobranie and a long tortoiseshell cigarette holder, and puffs away chatting to whoever is nearest him – me, today.

'Hello glamour!' he says – that's me – 'come and talk to us, darling. I expect you'll have heard of me? Quentin

Crisp, the dancer. What's your name then?' People laugh, but I like him and he is marvellous to draw, although today nothing I do seems to do him justice. Gerry turns out one of his fuzzy pencil Bonnard studies, Nick produces a careful, exquisite study of a touchingly beautiful young man's body in the Donatello or Da Vinci style. How does he do it? A real Renaissance draughtsman!

Ma thinks she may have found a house, near the Heath and not far from shops either. It has sitting tenants and some war damage, but not too bad. We are going to look at it soon.

Stuart Feldtman, one of the second-year students at Chelsea, is having a twenty-first birthday party tonight at his parents' flat and has invited me – I don't know why. Apparently, his father is a lord and incredibly rich, so everyone I know is going (they all want to eat the food and see the lord's very grand flat in Cavendish Square).

Stuart is overweight, can't draw, and wears a beret – to show that he is an 'artist', I suppose. He has a girlfriend, though, Lady Jane Somebody. She can't draw either, and looks like a greyhound – fast and beautiful – with a similar-sized brain.

I had thought that most of Cavendish Square was more or less a bomb site – bombs have fallen all along Oxford Street and on the John Lewis building – but actually the buildings containing the Feldtman flat have remained unscathed. Big rooms on the first floor, soft lights, parquet floors and large sofas covered in what looks like white leather.

A butler person lets us in and takes our coats, and a waiter offers us champagne. Someone in evening dress called Peter is playing muffled 'Palm Court' sort of music on the piano. The Feldtman father and his cronies are all in evening dress, too, and Stuart's mother, who is as broad as she is tall, is in some sort of fluffy creation which makes her look like a giant meringue. Poor fat Stuart is wearing a kilt! The rest of us, mostly art students, are in anything we can get hold of. I wear my slinky evening dress – black sort of crushed satin stuff, no sleeves just straps, made out of something that looked like blackout material in Great Aunt Nelly's trunk. With the cream velvet bed jacket and dangly earrings, it looks all right. (My friend Nina says it's a sensation!)

Red in the face, Stuart introduces everyone to his parents – then the piano strikes up and we start dancing. Everything goes OK for a while, as we either dance or chat and the piano player – who is somebody called Peter Ustinov and is an entertainer and friend of the family, it seems – tells jokes and larks about, and does very funny impersonations which make everybody laugh. (Easy when you are full to the brim with champagne!) Dinner next, and there is so much food that I have difficulty deciding what to put on my plate. I am standing looking at it all, when one of the other guests comes sidling up behind me. 'I would recommend the salmon for this beautiful young lady,' he says. 'Let me help you... My name is Roland...Harry Roland.'

He is plumpish and small with a bold rosy face, full red lips and black curls, the sort that can't keep their hands to themselves – you can see at a glance. He tells me he is going to open a gallery soon – am I painter? Oh, how much he would like to see my paintings, etc., etc. Art student, I say, putting a hunk of salmon on my plate.

He is now standing close behind me while I am trying to squirm away, but can't; people are crowding round to help themselves to food, and he's got me wedged against the table, hand sliding its way down my back until he gets to my bottom. He has a good feel around and then pinches me, twice! But I have had this sort of thing before, and I step back sharply and, with my very high pointed heel, stamp down as hard as I possibly can on his beautiful black polished toe. There's a gasp behind me and I turn round to see him doubled up, hopping about on one leg.

'Oh, sorry,' I say. 'Did I step on your foot?'

The salmon is delicious and I am coming back for more, when in the corner of the room I see Taffy Williams – a painter from the year above me – suddenly pour his glass of champagne over another student, whereupon a fight breaks out.

Taffy, completely drunk, and the other student go at it hammer and tongs but are separated finally, and Gerry and Nick pull him offstage somewhere, a bedroom, to cool down. When Nick goes back ten minutes later, Taffy has climbed into the large double bed, and is fast asleep! The rest of us go on dancing, and when Nick reappears I dance with him. The champagne flows, everything is fine and we are happily smooching round when the butler person comes hurrying in. He is followed by a uniformed policeman who says something to Stuart's father, who immediately looks exceedingly agitated. The music stops, and everyone looks at Lord F – who holds up his hand to get our attention, which of course he has already.

'No need for panic, but I have some, ah…bad news, I'm afraid. I very much regret to say that, ah…an unexploded bomb has been found in the basement of the adjoining property, and, ah…the police are urging us to clear the building immediately. So…very unfortunately, ah…I am, ah…going have to ask everyone to leave as quickly as possible…' Then the butler person tells us that if there's anybody unable to get home, there is room for a very few guests in the family Rolls waiting outside, which will be driving in a Knightsbridge direction very shortly. For anybody else, Lord F would be more than happy to hire taxis. Just send the invoice to his lordship's secretary…

Out in the street, the road is already cordoned off – police and firemen everywhere. The family appear, and climb into a large Rolls-Royce parked by the kerb. (A Silver Ghost, Nick tells me later.) Gerry, who is living in Putney, gets in too, plus one or two others and, with the hilarious Peter Ustinov driving, they leave. Mr Roland is still prowling around, but Nick appears suddenly and offers to take me home on the back of a motorbike he's borrowed from somewhere. Off we go with my beautiful evening gown wrapped up round my knees under his too big duffle coat, hair streaming in the wind. It is only when I am home that I suddenly remember Taffy, who I suppose is still sleeping soundly in someone's bed in Cavendish Square.

In the morning I listen to the news, but there's nothing about any unexploded bombs going off in central London. (Later, I heard that the bomb disposal people had been in while Taffy was still asleep, dismantled the bomb, and then left. And when he woke he was none the wiser!)

Ma and Julyan have gone to Uncle Christopher's, so this afternoon we are going to make some fireworks to take to a fireworks party that we have all been invited to. This, of course, means gunpowder – Simon's favourite substance. (The only time he was caned at his school was for making gunpowder. In the end, he and his pals took to making it in the photo darkroom because it was the only room in the school that locked from the inside.)

We find some newspaper and get out the jars of chemicals; Simon lights the Bunsen burner and soon the kitchen, doors tight shut because of draughts, is full of fumes from his foul-smelling glue. We make the fireworks by winding newspaper round a broom handle, gluing it all together and then chopping it up into convenient rolls. Then I stick a layer of drawing paper over this and paint and decorate it. Finally, Simon pours his magic mixture into the middle. With the fuses in place and painted bright yellow, blue, red, purple, orange, a bit of glitter and gold here and there, they look quite impressive. Proper crackers, in fact.

We've thought of some terrific names – Moon Rocket, Galactic Racer, Firewhizzer, things like that – which I am painting on in curly bright pink capital letters, outlined in black, on the outside of each firework.

Simon is making the last few fuses, short strips of newspaper dipped in saltpetre – i.e. potassium nitrate, which is what gunpowder is made from. While he's doing this, I collect all the finished fireworks together on the kitchen table, so I can admire them. I am still admiring them when I notice a slight smell of something burning, and suddenly there are a few sparks, some spasmodic bangs and – hallelujah! – all our lovely crackers start going off, ricocheting round the poor little kitchen like angry hornets. What to do? Water? No bucket, of course. After some dithering we manage to pull a blanket off my bed next door, and chuck it over everything. Quite loud explosions go on for several minutes, but gradually it calms down.

'A spark from the Bunsen burner must have ignited some of the loose gunpowder on the table,' Simon says calmly. 'Anyway, they worked OK.' (He seems quite pleased!)

In the end, we find that eight of the ones without fuses have survived, the others have all burned away to nothing; bits of charred paper and ash everywhere. The kitchen looks a mess…well, worse than a mess, and the blanket is a goner.

There is a lot of smoke hanging about, so I open the kitchen window and then our front door for a through draft. Very soon, Mrs Jackson from the flat downstairs walks in, saying she can smell smoke. In fact, now that she is in the flat she can *see* smoke – is there something on fire?

'No, no!' I hear Simon say. 'Everything's fine…'

'Your faces are completely *black*,' she says.

We look in the mirror and it's true – they are completely black – so we wash our faces and sweep up the ash and burnt paper, etc., put that and the blanket in the dustbin downstairs. But it takes us the rest of the afternoon to clean up the kitchen, wash the scorch marks and soot off everything, and I find myself thinking it's the last time. Really, we should have grown out of this sort of thing…

When Ma and Julyan arrive home, Ma looks at us as if she knows that something has happened but is not sure what.

'The whole flat smells…of…smoke,' she says, wrinkling her nose and looking hard at Simon then at me. 'And that glue. What have you been doing?'

'We made a few crackers,' I say, 'only…'

'…we ran out of gunpowder,' Simon adds, showing her the fireworks that we've got left.

'Nice colours,' Ma says, 'but you haven't made very many.'

In the end we go to the party with the eight rescued fireworks and some sparklers that Uncle Christopher had given Julyan.

'What's happened to your eyebrows, Simon?' somebody asks. And it occurs to me that probably we are lucky to have any hair left, let alone eyebrows.

Number seven Cannon Place is in a quiet street just off Heath Street, with the Heath and the Vale of Health round the corner, literally. It is nothing much to look at – yellowish-grey London brick and very run down – but it has got five floors if you count the two attic floors at the top occupied by an elderly refugee couple, sitting tenants. There is some bomb damage, I don't know how bad.

The front steps up to the raised ground floor look imposing, although the paint on the front door has almost peeled off, so it has jammed from the damp and is almost impossible to open. But finally we troop in and start to explore. First we walk through two spacious connecting rooms on the 'raised ground floor'. Both have beautiful wood parquet floors and views over a big wild garden at the back. Above these rooms are two bedrooms and an Edwardian bathroom, a ferocious geyser roaring in the corner. At the bottom of the house, we find a large rather gloomy basement, in which there is a kitchen and a number of subterranean rooms.

'Space for a workshop,' Simon murmurs, as we walk back up the stairs.

'Lovely parties in here when we open up the connecting doors,' I say, waltzing round on the parquet.

'But look at those cracks in the ceiling! Is that the bomb damage?' Ma's face is apprehensive and happy at the same time. 'If I go ahead, you will all have to help.' She shakes her head. 'A lot needs doing... We'll see what the surveyor has to say. Where's Julyan?'

'Hanging out of the window upstairs talking to the girls opposite,' Simon says. 'Did you notice their dad's 1930 Lagonda in the street?'

Slightly breathless, Julyan comes tumbling in to the room.

'Smashing blonde over the road,' he says. 'Are we going to live here?'

Chelsea Art School is taking part in the Chelsea Arts Ball this year. The theme is the Renaissance, and each school is designing a float linked to the art of the period to show their skills and give an idea of the Renaissance.

Our float is to be based on Botticelli's Venus being transported across the sea on a shell. John's girlfriend, Annette, has agreed to be Venus – nude like the original, with a few strategic veils; a red-headed sculpture student has offered to be the figure of Spring welcoming her, and eternal windbag John the figure of the wind blowing her across the sea. The rest of us, dressed as Renaissance Florentines of one sort and another, are to drape ourselves next to her while pushing the float round the central arena of the Albert Hall. I am going as a Florentine page: bobbed page boy hair, long red silk stockings like tights, black velvet tunic with dangling scarlet sleeves, and a white starched ruff. We have several rehearsals, and all is going well when, at the last minute, Annette falls off the float and breaks her arm and says she can't do it. Panic and despair as nobody else wants to volunteer! In the end, John persuades her to change her mind, and she says she will if, as well as the plaster cast, she can wear a G-string.

On the night, we all meet to get dressed up in someone's flat in the King's Road, and in due course set off for the Albert Hall. I have seen crowds at the Albert Hall before at concerts, but not in fancy dress, and actually it almost feels like being back in Botticelli's Florence. Minesweeper Nick has got himself up as a pope, in red velvet and furs, and is so dignified and grand he is unrecognisable – until he lifts up his skirts and starts jiving and jitterbugging around, mitre over one eye and shaking his legs and generally playing the fool. I thought I was going to die laughing. I recognise various historical figures: the Mona Lisa, Da Vinci himself, assorted madonnas and angels, and a magnificent doge looking as if he's come straight off a gondola on the Grand Canal. Everyone is excited and friendly (and fairly drunk). We push our wobbly float round the central promenade section, and Annette gets roars of approval and a lot of clapping in her G-string and plaster cast. Then it is dancing, more wine and crowds and crowds of happy people. I dance with everyone who asks me, and meet a chemistry student from Paris, Freddy, who is feeling bad because he's not in fancy dress and he's failed his exams and daren't go home to face his furious father. I say he can stay with us if he's homeless, and scribble the address on his shirt cuff.

Then Nick appears, having shed most of his pope outfit, and I forget all about Freddy, forget about everything. Nick and I dance until we are almost the only couple left and the orchestra is beginning to pack up. Together we wander north through a sleeping London, across the park and Grosvenor Square, Baker Street, Regent's Park and the Regent's Canal – it seems no distance – then sit on a bench near the zoo to watch the first streaks of dawn, and at first light fortify ourselves with coffee from an all-night taxi stand. After many lingering 'goodbyes' (of course Nick wants to come in with me, but I say no, not here, not now, my watchdog mother will bite you in half then throw you out), we agree to meet later today and I creep into the silent flat and bed.

My feet are cold and sore and the sheets are like ice, but I lie there smiling and thinking how ridiculously happy I am. All on account of a dancing pope who draws like Da Vinci, the magic of walking through a peaceful London at night with the one person you want to be with. (Sudden thought: in six weeks it will be my birthday. Another party?) Mmm, life is good, big smile. Down I go, drifting into sleep, wake with a jump as – *bang bang bang!* – someone is thumping on my cupboard bedroom door.

'Marjorie-Ann are you awake? A friend of yours – Freddy? – is asleep on the sitting room floor. Look after him, please? And make sure Julyan gets some breakfast when you have yours dear, will you? Porridge perhaps? Must go, I am late. *Marjorie-Ann!* Are you awake?'

Groaning something in reply, I listen to Ma clattering round getting ready for work, then the front door clicks and all is quiet. I turn over and go to sleep.

Ma has bought the house in Cannon Place! The initial deposit has been paid to the solicitor, and in six weeks she will give him the rest of it, and the house will be ours. I can hardly believe it, and I don't think she can either. She wants to move in at New Year, so today, as it's a Saturday, she and I have been in to visit and measure for curtains, bookshelves, decide which rooms to paint first and what colours. I am going to have one of the big rooms with the parquet flooring and she will have the other one, as bed-sitting rooms. We'll keep the connecting folding doors shut, with a thick curtain across them most of the time, but open them up for parties. And at last I will have a room big enough for my easel. Thankfully the boys will be downstairs, and Simon can have a workshop down there too. Then she'll let the two bedrooms upstairs to pay the mortgage. It all works fine.

There is no heating, inside or out, and anyway the light is going, so we decide we have done enough for one day and start walking back across the Heath to Belsize Park.

The gun emplacements and the barrage balloons have all gone. Nothing left to see there now except scuffed scooped-out hollows, the blanched white grass already turning green. Swans patrol the dark water of the ice-fringed ponds where Keats once walked (probably), and ducks and coots are gathering hoping to be fed. It seems impossible that soon we will be living in our own house and will be able to walk out here whenever we want! Suddenly I feel wonderfully happy and calm, hopeful, as if everything is going to be all right now in the best of all possible worlds. I am a painter – or I soon will be. I am nineteen, in love, invincible. Nothing can go wrong now.

'It will be different! Another sort of life,' Ma says. 'An ending of something and a beginning of something else–' she halts abruptly, gazing at me with a worried face. 'I just hope I am doing the right thing?'

'Of course you are!' I say without thinking twice.

'It *is* very exciting!' She looks suddenly young and extremely cheerful, and leans forward to hug me. 'Let's celebrate for once! See if we can find some doughnuts for tea!' And we jig round laughing and giggling, hugging each other. 'Race you to the ponds!' Ma shouts suddenly, taking me by surprise. We chase each other downhill across the tussocky grass like a couple of children – I had no idea she could run so fast – and then, out of breath and still laughing, walk on past the ducks and swans, towards the lights from the shops which are beginning to twinkle and glow in the dusk.

'Pot of tea for two and some doughnuts, please,' Ma says when we are in the tea room. 'And do you have any chocolate cake?' When the waitress brings the plate piled with doughnuts *and* chocolate cake, and Ma has poured out the tea, she holds up her cup. 'To the future!' she says. We clink our cups together and drink our tea, smiling like two Cheshire cats.

The future, I think. Yes, finally, the future is beginning.

Author's Note

After graduating from Cambridge University with a degree in civil engineering, Simon emigrated to Canada and got a job designing timber bridges for forest access roads in the interior of the province. He moved to Montreal to work for the Aluminium Company of Canada (ALCAN), and then to Boston to enrol in the MIT School of Architecture. While still a student, he began designing and making furniture, moving eventually to Vermont to build a house for himself and family there, and set up a furniture-making business. He then began building traditional wooden boats and spent several years travelling round North America teaching small groups the basics of clinker boat building. Eventually, he moved to San Francisco to combine boat building, teaching and making furniture, and has written several books on these subjects. He lives in San Francisco during the winter, and an island home in Nova Scotia in summer.

Julyan continued with the violin, studied music at the Guildhall, then won a scholarship to study modern languages at King's College, Cambridge. At thirty-three he qualified as a chartered accountant, and moved to Vienna in charge of Ernst and Young's audit operations. IIASA than appointed him as its first director of finance and administration. He is fluent in German, French, Polish, and Russian, and has worked for the United Nations, the European Commission and the World Bank as an international expert in government finance and audit, spending several years in the former Soviet republics of Central Asia. His latest major project has been the creation of a national audit office in Tajikistan. He lives in Hungary.

Acknowledgements

I would like to thank all my family for their love and encouragement, and Jane Turnbull, my friend and agent, without whom this book would not have been published.